Anonymous

The Fredonia Cook Book

Anonymous

The Fredonia Cook Book

ISBN/EAN: 9783744781329

Printed in Europe, USA, Canada, Australia, Japan

Cover: Foto ©Lupo / pixelio.de

More available books at **www.hansebooks.com**

THE
FREDONIA COOK BOOK.

COMPILED BY THE LADIES OF THE TRINITY
PARISH GUILD.

FREDONIA CENSOR PRINT.
1899.

Preface.

The committee appointed by Trinity Parish Guild, for the purpose of compiling this cook book, present it to the public with the earnest wish that it may be of practical use in many households. The recipes have been gathered from different sources, and it is believed that they are all reliable and practical. It is not claimed that this book is an exhaustive compilation of recipes for cooking; but it contains many suggestions which will be acceptable as a supplement to other cook books; and it will add to the knowledge already possessed by many who are experienced cooks.

We are pleased in this place to thank those who have taken space in this book for advertisements, for their prompt responses to letters and liberal orders. We take great pleasure in calling attention to the materials and goods mentioned in this volume. Their use will add to the success and value of the FREDONIA COOK BOOK.

Table of Weights and Measures.

4 teaspoonfuls of liquid	= 1 tablespoonful
4 tablespoonfuls of liquid	= ½ gill, ¼ cup, or 1 wineglassful
1 tablespoonful of liquid	= ½ ounce
1 pint of liquid	= 1 pound
2 gills of liquid	= 1 cup or ½ pint
1 kitchen cup	= ½ pint
1 heaping quart of sifted flour	= 1 pound
4 cups of flour	= 1 quart or 1 pound
1 rounded tablespoonful of flour	= ½ ounce
3 cups of corn meal	= 1 pound
1½ pints of corn meal	= 1 pound
1 cup of butter	= ½ pound
1 pint of butter	= 1 pound
1 tablespoonful of butter	= 1 ounce
Butter the size of an egg	= 2 ounces
Butter size of a walnut	= 1 ounce
1 solid pint of chopped meat	= 1 pound
10 eggs	= 1 pound
A dash of pepper	= ⅛ teaspoonful, 3 good shakes
2 cups of granulated sugar	= 1 pound
1 pint of granulated sugar	= 1 pound
1 pint of brown sugar	= 13 ounces
2½ cups of powdered sugar	= 1 pound

Soups.

STOCK FOR SOUP.

Graded Cook Book.

Allow 1 quart of cold water to a pound of meat. Let it stand awhile before putting it on the back of the stove. Cover and simmer slowly. Five hours are required for boiling a good sized bone. When done pour into an earthen vessel and skim when cold. If desired to keep several days leave the fat on until used. This fat may be clarified and used for cooking by putting into boiling water. When it cools all sediment will settle to the bottom and the fat can again be skimmed off. Salt the stock when half done. Vegetables can be added to the stock in the proportion of 1 pint cut vegetables to every gallon. The meat can be spiced and baked or made into hash or croquettes. If desired stronger, use 5 pounds of meat to 7 pints of water. When the stock begins to boil, throw in ½ cup of cold water and skim.

WHITE STOCK FOR SOUP.

Mrs. Jacobi.

Place in a large stock urn, on a moderate fire, a good heavy knuckle of fine white veal, with 2 pounds of good soup meat. Cover with cold water, add a handful of salt and when it comes to a boil skim all the scum off. Then add 2 large sound and well-scraped carrots, 1 sound white turnip, 1 large peeled onion (split carrots, turnip and onion in half), 1 well-cleaned parsley root, 3 thoroughly washed

Something modern—Virot's Extracts.

leeks, and a few leaves of cleaned celery. Boil very slowly for six hours on corner of the range. Carefully skim the grease off, strain well through a wet cloth into a large earthen bowl, and put away in a cool place for general use.

ASPARAGUS SOUP.
Mrs. Joseph Brown.

2 quarts chicken stock.
2 bunches of asparagus.
2 tablespoons of butter.
1 quart of milk.
Just as much flour as the butter will dissolve.

Cut the heads off the asparagus and save in a cup; cut up stalks and put in stock and boil one hour.

Boil heads in 1 cup of salted water. Melt butter and flour in a stew pan and stir in milk until it cooks; strain stock; stir in strained milk, butter, etc., and season thoroughly with salt and pepper. Before serving put in ½ cup of cream and asparagus heads.

BLACK BEAN SOUP.
Mrs. A. R. Moore.

1 pint of black beans, soaked over night in 3 quarts of water. In the morning pour off this water and add 3 quarts of fresh.

Boil gently 2 hours. When done there should be 1 quart. Add a quart of stock, 2 whole cloves, 2 whole allspice, a small piece of mace, a small piece of cinnamon, a stalk of celery and a small onion. Into a frying pan put 3 tablespoonfuls of butter, and when it begins to bubble add 1 tablespoonful of flour and cook until brown. Add to soup and simmer all together 1 hour. Season with salt and pepper and rub through a fine sieve. Serve with slices of lemon and hard boiled eggs.

Just before taking from the stove add ½ teacup of wine.

Better than the Best—Virot's Extracts.

CELERY SOUP.
Mrs. A. S. Fox.

4 bunches of celery.
1 pint of good soup stock.
3 pints of water.
½ pint of cream.

Cut the celery into inch lengths, put on with the water and cook until tender. Take out the celery and rub through a sieve, add to the soup stock and cook slowly ½ hour. Heat the cream and stir into it 1 tablespoonful of flour rubbed into 1 tablespoonful of butter; pour into the celery; let cook till very hot, but not boil, and serve at once.

CLAM CHOWDER.
Mrs. Burritt.

20 large clams, 4 large onions, 4 potatoes, ½ pound salt pork chopped fine, ½ can tomatoes, 1 heaping teaspoonful of thyme, 1 heaping tablespoonful Worcestershire sauce (just before serving), pepper to taste, 1½ large hard-tack broken in before serving.

Chop the clams fine, place in kettle with liquor and 1½ quarts of water, let come to a boil and skim; then add the other ingredients; have them all chopped fine; let simmer slowly all day. If too thick add hot water.

CLAM CHOWDER.
Mrs. MacDonald Moore.

2 dozen clams, 6 potatoes, 5 onions.

Chop 2 slices of salt pork very fine and fry brown. Put in bottom of pot a little of fried pork, then successive layers of sliced onions, sliced potatoes and clams. Pour in clam liquor and add sufficient water to cover them; season highly with cayenne pepper and a little salt. Cook until potatoes are done, then add 1 pint of hot milk and boil slowly 3 hours. Just before serving, add 1 cup of cream and 2 large spoons of butter.

Pure, delicate, strong—Virot's Extracts.

CLAM CHOWDER.
Miss Heyl.

25 clams, ½ pound salt pork, 1 quart milk, 6 medium sized potatoes, 4 medium sized onions, 1 can of corn, 1 tablespoonful butter, 2 tablespoonfuls flour, 4 sea biscuits.

Wash clams thoroughly with brush. Put in kettle with 2 quarts boiling water. When shells open, remove the clams from them; cut in small pieces. Cut the pork in small pieces and fry until light brown; add onions, chopped fine. When cooked, turn into kettle of clam water; then add the potatoes cut in cubes. When potatoes are half done, add clams; cook till potatoes are done, add milk; when it boils, add corn and butter and flour (cooked together in spider). Let this boil up once; add crackers, broken in pieces. Set on back of stove; lastly, add the yolk of 1 egg, and season with salt and cayenne pepper.

CORN SOUP.
Miss Jennie Prescott.

Put 1 can of corn and 1 pint of milk into a double boiler and boil ½ hour. Strain and add 1 cup strong stock; season with salt and a little red pepper; thicken with one large spoonful of flour, worked well into 1 spoonful of butter (if it is the least lumpy strain again). Just as you take it off stir in quickly 1 pint of whipped cream.

You can use peas or celery in the same way.

JULIENNE SOUP.
Mrs. MacDonald Moore.

Make a brown beef stock; let it get cold, and remove all grease. Fry 1 carrot in butter, put it into the stock with 1 small onion, 1 slice of turnip, 1 beet and a little cabbage; let it boil 40 minutes. Add the juice of half a lemon before serving.

Equaled by none—Virot's Extracts.

SALSIFY SOUP.

Mrs. Pratt.

1 bunch salsify, 2 quarts water. Cook until done. Add 1 cup milk, 2 tablespoonfuls of butter, 1 teaspoonful of flour, salt and pepper. Strain and serve.

MULLAGATAWNY SOUP.

Mrs. W. B. Greer.

Cut 4 onions, 1 carrot, 2 turnips, 1 head of celery, into 3 quarts of liquor in which one or two fowls have been boiled. Keep it over a brisk fire until it boils, then place it on a corner of fire and let it simmer 20 minutes. Add 1 tablespoonful of curry powder and 1 tablespoonful of flour; mix the whole well together and let it boil three minutes; pass it through a colander. Serve with pieces of roast chicken in it. It must be good yellow color, and if too thick you can add a little boiling water and a teaspoonful of sugar. Half veal and half chicken will answer as well.

OYSTER SOUP.

Mrs. H. Hargis.

Drain the liquor from 1 quart of oysters; add this to 1 quart of milk. When this reaches the boiling point, add 1 tablespoonful of butter. When melted add the oysters, leaving them only until they curl; when add ½ teacup of cream and ½ teacup of rolled crackers. Season with salt and pepper. Do not add water.

ONION SOUP.

Mrs. Jacobi.

Chop 2 onions very fine and brown in a sauce pan with a piece of butter the size of 2 eggs; stir in 2 tablespoons (heaping) of sifted flour. Be careful not to burn. Add slowly 3 pints of white broth; mix thoroughly and smoothly; season with salt and pepper to taste; cook for 10 minutes. Place 6 pieces of toasted bread in a large bowl; cover them

For fastidious tastes—Virot's Extracts.

with very thin slices of Swiss cheese; pour the soup over them; add 2 tablespoonfuls of Swiss cheese, cut in very small and thin pieces. Put in the oven 5 minutes before serving.

This quantity is enough for six or eight people.

SPLIT PEA SOUP.

Mrs. Swetland.

Wash 1 pint of split peas and cover them with cold water, adding ¼ teaspoonful of soda. Let them stand over night to swell. Next morning put them in a kettle with close fitting cover. Pour over them 3 quarts of cold water, adding ½ pound of lean ham or bacon, cut into small pieces; also a teaspoonful of salt, a little pepper and some celery, chopped fine, if you like. When the soup begins to boil, skim the surface; cook it slowly 3 or 4 hours—until the peas are all dissolved—adding more boiling water, to keep the quantity as it boils away. Strain through a colander; serve very hot with lemon sliced fine, or toasted bread cut in squares.

If not rich enough, add butter and season to taste. It should be quite thick when served. This soup can be made without the meat and celery. Season with butter, salt and pepper, and serve with croutons.

VEGETABLE SOUP.

Mrs. E. K. Cherry.

2 pounds of soup meat, 1 large sized onion, 1 bunch of celery, 1 large potato, small piece of carrot, a little parsley, 1 can strained tomatoes, ½ cup of rice, salt and pepper.

Boil the meat 4 hours, and set away until next day. Remove grease and put in rice; let it cook on back of stove. Chop onion, celery, potato, carrot and parsley, and cook separately until done. Pour into the broth with 1 can of tomatoes, and cook on the front of stove.

For dainty toilets—Virot's Perfumes, Toilet Waters, Sachets.

POTATO SOUP.

Mrs. Pratt.

1 quart of milk.
3 hot boiled potatoes.
A very little chopped onion, or Virot's extract of onion, to taste.
1 tablespoonful butter.

Boil the milk and onion together; cream the potatoes; stir into the hot milk, and thicken a very little with flour. Strain the whole before serving.

TOMATO SOUP.

Mrs. S. G. Skinner.

Place a pint of tomatoes on the stove to cook, and keep them boiling until wanted. About 10 minutes before dinner place a large tablespoonful of butter in a frying pan, and when it is melted put into it a tablespoonful of flour, stirring until thoroughly cooked, but not browned. Into the tomatoes stir ½ teaspoonful of soda, salt and pepper; add to the butter and flour, then pour into the whole 1 pint of milk. Strain all through a wire sieve and serve very hot.

CLEAR TOMATO SOUP.

"The Columbia."

1 quart of tomatoes.
1 quart white stock or water.
1 dozen cloves.
1 small onion.
1 bunch of parsley.
1 tablespoonful of sugar.
Salt to taste.

Boil together for 1 hour in porcelain or agate kettle. Strain through fine sieve. Put back into kettle and add 1 tablespoonful of cornstarch, rubbed into a smooth paste with cold water, and a piece of butter size of an egg. Season with cayenne or black pepper.

Demand and Get—Virot's Perfumes and Extracts.

Fish and Oysters.

Boil large fish; bake medium sized ones; fry small ones. Fish cooks in from 5 to 15 minutes to the pound, according to thickness.

BOILED FISH.

Salmon should be put on to boil in salt water when boiling; also bass and rock fish. To a gallon of water put four tablespoonfuls of salt, and a wineglass of vinegar to give it firmness. To boil other fish: if a common kettle is used, lay the fish on a plate, run a skewer through to hold the head and tail together; wrap all in a napkin and cover with cold water. When done take out by lifting the cloth; serve on a hot platter garnished with lemon and parsley, or anything desired.

TO BAKE FISH.

Stuff with plain bread stuffing, made of ½ pint of bread crumbs, 1 tablespoonful of butter, small spoon of salt and pepper each, 1 tablespoonful of parsley. Work all together and moisten, if necessary, with egg. Fill and tie in shape with a string. Wash the roe, if any, and cook with the fish.

FISH CUTLETS.

Mrs. Rorer,

½ pint of milk; 3 teaspoonfuls of Cottolene; three even tablespoonfuls flour; 1 egg yolk; 1 tablespoonful parsley, chopped; ¼ grated nutmeg; 10 drops onion juice; 2 cups of cold boiled fish; seasoning.

Price to suit all—Virot's Products.

Put the milk on to boil. Rub together the Cottolene and flour; then stir them into the boiling milk; stir and cook until a thick paste is formed, add the yolk of egg, parsley, onion juice; mix and add the boiled fish; mix again and add a palatable seasoning of salt and cayenne; turn out to cool. When cold, form into cutlets or croquettes. Dip first in beaten egg, then in bread crumbs, and fry in very hot Cottolene. Drain on brown paper and serve very hot with cream sauce.

SALMON LOAF.

Mrs. R. H. Barnum.

1 can of salmon.
5 tablespoonfuls of butter.
4 eggs.
½ cup of bread crumbs; salt and pepper to taste.

Shred the salmon and mix with the butter, which has been beaten light. Eggs beaten and mixed with the crumbs. Then mix all together. Butter a mould, and steam 1 hour.

SAUCE.

1 cup of milk and oil from the salmon; 1 tablespoonful of butter. Let these come to a boil, and thicken with a teaspoonful of cornstarch. 1 egg beaten and stirred in at the last; with a pinch of cayenne pepper and 1 teaspoonful of catsup at the last.

FISH TURBOT.

Mrs. Joseph Brown.

Take white-fish or halibut, 4 pounds at least; boil in salt water about 5 minutes; when free from bones, have ready the following dressing:

1 large spoonful of butter.
1 scant spoonful of flour.
1 pint of milk. Season highly, to taste.

Dissolve the butter in the sauce pan; stir in flour until smooth and foamy; pour in cold milk and stir until it

Something modern—Virot's Extracts.

thickens. Butter a dish, sprinkle in a few bread crumbs; then put a layer of fish, then a layer of cream dressing, and so on, having the top layer of cream. Sprinkle bread crumbs and tiny bits of butter on top. Bake 20 minutes. Should be brown on top.

CODFISH BALLS.
Graded Cook Book.

1 pint of potatoes, peeled; 1 scant pint of fish, picked fine. Boil together. When done, drain off water and beat together well; add butter size of an egg; a little pepper and 1 egg, well beaten. Drop in hot lard and fry.

MINCED FISH.
Mrs. A. R. Moore,

1 quart of cold fish, carefully flaked.
1 pint of milk or cream.
1 can of mushrooms, cut in half.
2 tablespoonfuls of butter.
2 tablespoonfuls of flour.

Put the butter in a frying pan to melt, being careful not to brown; when melted, add the flour and mix well, then add the milk or cream; stir continually until it boils. Add mushrooms and liquor, and pour this over the minced fish, and mix carefully. Salt and pepper to taste. Put all in a pan and grate cheese over the top. Place in an oven and allow to brown.

LOBSTER CROQUETTES.
Mrs. S. H. Quinby.

Take two lobsters and chop the meat fine. Put in a sauce pan; butter size of an egg and 2 tablespoonfuls of flour, rubbed in. Add to this enough milk or cream to make a creamy substance. Add the chopped lobster, and

Better than the Best—Virot's Extracts.

let all come to a boil. Season with salt and a little cayenne pepper and lemon juice. Shape when cool; roll in egg and cracker crumbs; fry a nice brown. Drain on brown or blotting paper.

OYSTERS WITH BROWN SAUCE.

Mrs. Barrett-Howard.

25 oysters.
1 pint of stock.   1 tablespoonful of onion juice.
1 tablespoonful of butter.   2 tablespoonfuls of cream.
1 tablespoonful of flour.   Salt and cayenne pepper to taste.

Boil the oysters in their own liquor; drain; melt and brown the butter; add the flour, and mix until smooth. Add the stock (made from the bones of turkey or chicken), and oysters, onion juice, cream and seasoning. Stir until thoroughly heated. Serve on rounds of toast dipped in melted butter. Garnish with thin slices of lemon, sprinkled with parsley.

FRIED OYSTERS.

Miss Parloa.

Oysters for frying should be large and plump. Spread them on a towel to drain, and after seasoning them with pepper and salt, roll them in fine dry bread or cracker crumbs. Have Cottolene about 4 inches deep in the frying kettle, and when hot, test as directed: Cover the bottom of the frying-basket with a single layer of breaded oysters and plunge into the fat. Cook for 1½ minutes. Drain and serve immediately. For a dozen and a half of oysters, there will be required 2 eggs, ¼ teaspoonful pepper, 1 level tablespoonful of salt, and 1 pint of crumbs. Use ½ the salt and pepper to season the oysters, and the rest to season the crumbs. If the flavor be liked, 2 tablespoonfuls of tomato catsup may be mixed with egg. Remember that there are few things that require the fat so hot as oysters, or that spoil so quickly if allowed to stand after frying.

Pure, delicate, strong—Virot's Extracts.

SOUTHERN SHRIMP AND OYSTER GUMBO.
Mrs. Jacobi.

Chop a medium sized onion very fine; also a medium sized green pepper. Place in a sauce pan with a piece of butter the size of an egg, and a little raw, lean ham, cut in small pieces. Let cook for 5 minutes, being careful the onions don't burn; then add the shrimps. Toss on stove a minute or so; then add 1 quart of stock (if there is no home-made stock handy, a can of Franco-American Consomme will answer.) Add 3 or 4 tablespoonfuls of canned okra, if the green okra is not to be had. Let boil for 15 minutes; then add 1 pint of oysters; and, while the gumbo is boiling add slowly, by sprinkling in, 2 tablespoonfuls of the Gumbo File; stir constantly until there are no lumps. Serve very hot. and with boiled rice, cooked Southern style—each kernel to itself. Excellent.

OYSTER CROQUETTES.
Mrs. Louis McKinstry.

25 oysters.
1 tablespoonful of chopped parsley.
½ cup of oyster liquor
½ cup of cream.
¼ of a nutmeg, grated.
1 tablespoonful of butter.
2 tablespoonfuls of flour.
Salt and cayenne pepper to taste.

Put the oysters to boil in their own liquor; boil and stir constantly for a few minutes. Take from the fire and drain. Chop the oysters very fine. Now put ½ cup of this liquor and the cream into a sauce pan. Rub together the butter and the flour and add this and the oysters to the boiling liquor, and cream and stir until it boils and thickens. Add the yolks of 2 eggs; stir over the fire 1 minute. Take it off, add the parsley, salt, cayenne pepper and nutmeg; mix well and turn out to cool. When cold form into cylinders; roll first in beaten egg, then in bread crumbs, and fry in boiling hot fat.

Equaled by none—Virot's Extracts.

CREAMED OYSTERS.

Miss Grace McKinstry.

1 quart of oysters.
1 cup of cream.

Put the liquor and cream in a sauce pan, bringing to the boiling point. Thicken with 1 tablespoonful of flour and 1 of butter. Put in the oysters and cook until they begin to curl. Add pepper and salt, and turn over toast or into patty cases.

ESCALLOPED OYSTERS.

Mrs. H. J. Commons.

Fill a buttered dish with alternate layers of oysters and grated crackers or bread crumbs. Season each layer with butter, pepper and salt. Have a thick layer of crumbs on top; moisten with a little cream or rich milk. Bake about 45 minutes. Brown on top.

OYSTER COCKTAIL.

Place four small oysters in a glass; add 1 tablespoonful of oyster liquor, 1 tablespoonful of lemon juice, the same of tomato catsup, a dash of tobasco sauce, ¼ even teaspoonful of salt and a very little pepper; add some finely shaved ice and 1 teaspoonful of horseradish, finely grated. Serve with an oyster fork.

Meats.

BRICK OF BEEF.
Mrs. Lambert.

3½ pounds of lean beef, chopped fine.
4 crackers, rolled.
3 eggs, well beaten.
Salt and pepper to taste.
A little celery salt or seed.

Mix well, mould into a brick; cover with bits of salt pork and rolled bread crumbs; put a coffeecup of water in the pan. Bake 1 hour. Baste often.

BEEF OMELET.
Mrs. M. M. Fenner.

2 pounds of beefsteak, clear beef, chopped fine.
4 soda crackers, rolled fine.
4 eggs, beaten.
½ cup of butter.
½ cup of milk.

Salt and pepper to taste; small onion, chopped fine, and a pinch of sage.

Mix in chopping bowl, and make into two loaves. Put in a covered pan, with 2 cups of water to each loaf. Bake in a moderate oven ¾ or 1 hour.

TONGUE DE TERRAPIN.
Mrs. MacDonald Moore.

1 beef tongue, boiled until thoroughly done. Cut the large part of the tongue on one side and fill it with plain stuffing. Put in a pan and pour over it 1 quart of tomatoes.

For dainty toilets—Virot's Perfumes, Toilet Waters, Sachets.

Season with salt and cayenne pepper, and add 1 cup of sherry; bake in a slow oven 1 hour. Just before taking up, add a large spoonful of butter. Serve with sliced hard boiled eggs and lemon. Garnish the dish with parsley.

BOUDINS.
Mrs. H. D. Jarvis.

Chop cold cooked meat fine. To every pint, add:
1 tablespoonful of butter.
2 tablespoonfuls of dry bread crumbs.
½ cup of stock or boiling water.
2 eggs, slightly beaten. Salt and pepper to taste.

Put over the fire, and stir until thoroughly mixed. Fill custard cups with this mixture, ⅔ full; stand them in a baking pan ½ full of hot water, and bake 20 minutes. Turn them out carefully on a hot dish, and pour around them Cream or Bechamel sauce. Remains of cold roast or poultry are good served this way.

BAKED HAMBURG STEAK.
Mrs. Kate L. Cushing.

Take 1 egg, well beaten; mix well with 1 pound fresh Hamburg steak. Add ½ cup of bread crumbs; butter size of a walnut; salt and pepper. Form into a roll 2 inches thick, and bake ½ hour. A tablespoonful of water in the baking dish; baste occasionally. This is enough for four persons, and is fine, either hot or sliced cold for luncheon or tea.

VEAL LOAF.
Mrs. Burritt.

1½ pounds of veal.
¼ pound pork, chopped fine.
2 crackers. 2 eggs.
1 teaspoonful of salt.
Butter size of an egg. 1½ cups sweet milk.
Mix all well together and bake.

Demand and Get—Virot's Perfumes and Extracts.

VEAL CUTLETS.
Mrs. Lambert.

1 slice of veal from the leg. Remove the bone and tough membrane; cut into small pieces for serving. Sprinkle wih salt and pepper. Dip in beaten egg; then roll in fine bread crumbs. Fry until brown. Make a gravy of 1 tablespoonful of butter, 1 tablespoonful of flour, 1½ cups of water or stock. Season with salt and pepper. Pour over the cutlets, and simmer for 45 minutes.

SWEETBREADS FRIED.
Mrs. H. Hargis.

Prepare as for salad, only do not cut. Dip in egg and then in bread crumbs, and fry brown in butter. When done, prepare in a frying pan a large cup of sweet cream, a little pepper; dust in a very little flour; and when it boils up, pour over the sweet breads and serve very hot.

STEWED LIVER.
Mrs. C. M. Rathbun.

1 pound of calf's liver.　　1 pint of water.
1 tablespoonful of flour.　　1 small onion.
Salt and pepper to taste.

Cut the liver in slices, then again into pieces about 2 inches square. Put 2 tablespoonfuls of dripping into a pan; add to it the flour and stir until brown. Now add the water; stir constantly until it boils. Pour it into a stewing pan with the liver and onion; cover and simmer gently for 1 hour. Add salt and pepper, and serve.

ROAST TURKEY OR CHICKEN.
Mrs. Wm. Lester.

After the fowl is singed and cleaned, wash and dry quickly with a linen towel. Fill the inside, and sew up; then fill in at the neck, and draw the skin over the back and fasten.

Price to suit all—Virot's Products.

Fasten the legs and wings close to the body; also tie the lower ends of the legs together. Put enough water in the tin to keep it from burning; add a little salt; turn and baste often. Bake in a moderate oven, 15 minutes to the pound. The following is one rule for

TURKEY DRESSING.

Take first joint of wings, part of neck, the heart, liver and gizzard, and boil soft. When nearly done, add 5 or 6 potatoes. When all are boiled, remove bones chop and season with pepper and salt and a good sized piece of butter. Soak nearly a small loaf of bread in the water in which meat and potatoes were boiled; add to the dressing.

DRY DRESSING FOR TURKEY OR CHICKEN.

Graded Cook Book.

2 coffee cups of dry bread crumbs.
⅓ teacup of butter.
1 tablespoonful of parsley or sage.
1 teaspoonful of salt.
1 teaspoonful of black pepper.

Oysters, celery, onion, or any desired flavor can be used in the dressing instead of sage.

ROYAL SCALLOP.

Mrs. Sarah Cutler.

Boil a chicken tender, bone and chop fine. Add ¾ of a cupful of canned mushrooms, after they have been boiled; drain and chop fine. Boil 6 fresh eggs 20 minutes; then drop into cold water, to prevent the yolks from turning dark. While the eggs are boiling, prepare the sauce: Put into a double boiler 1 pint of sweet milk. Let it get boiling hot. Put into a sauce pan 2 spoonfuls of butter; when hot gradually smooth it with flour; then add the hot milk, ½ teaspoonful of salt and a salt spoon of white pepper. Cook a few minutes. Prepare 1 cupful of fine cracker crumbs, to

Something modern—Virot's Extracts.

which add ¼ cup of melted butter or thick cream. Separate the yolks and whites of the boiled eggs; chop the whites fine and rub the yolks through a sieve. Now well butter a scallop dish; put a layer of crumbs over the bottom, then a layer of whites of eggs. Cover these with 2 good tablespoonfuls of the white sauce; then same of the minced meat and the mushrooms, building up until all the materials prepared have been used, covering the top with cracker crumbs. Bake a good brown. Serve hot in the dish in which it has been cooked.

CHICKEN PILLAU.
Mrs. Wm. Shelton.

Boil a good sized fowl until tender, keeping covered with water, salted. Remove chicken from liquor, and season with black pepper and curry powder to taste. Clean and wash as much rice as desired; add to the liquor and stir constantly until most of the liquor is absorbed. Set on the back of stove and stir occasionally. Reserve a little of the liquor to make egg sauce for the chicken, as follows: Put a piece of butter in a sauce pan and stir in flour until smooth, then add the liquor; boil until it thickens. Then slice 1 or 2 hard boiled eggs, to put over chicken.

CREAMED CHICKEN.
Mrs. Selden E. Stone.

Slowly simmer until tender, 2 chickens, salting a little. Drain the chicken, and boil the liquor down to ½ pint. Cut the meat when cold into dice shapes. Drain a can of French mushrooms and cut them into quarters. Put into a sauce pan 1 large tablespoonful of butter; when melted, add 2 heaping tablespoonfuls of flour, stirring until smooth; then add cupful of broth and ½ pint of cream. Boil till done; then add the chicken and mushrooms. Season to taste. Cook in a double boiler.

Better than the Best—Virot's Extracts.

CHICKEN CROQUETTES.

Mrs. A. R. Moore.

3 small, or 2 large sweetbreads.
1 boiled chicken.
1 large tablespoonful of flour.
1 pint of cream.
½ cupful butter.
1 tablespoonful of onion juice.
1 tablespoonful of chopped parsley.
1 teaspoonful of mace.
Juice of ½ a lemon; salt and pepper to taste.

Let the sweetbreads stand in boiling water 10 minutes. Grind very fine with the chicken, and add seasoning. Put the butter in a stew pan with the flour; when it bubbles, add the cream gradually; then add the chopped mixture, and stir until thoroughly heated. Take from the fire, add the lemon juice and set away to cool. When cold, roll into shape. Dip into beaten eggs thinned with milk, then into cracker crumbs. Let them stand until dry, when dip again in eggs and finally into bread crumbs, not too fine. All the crumbs should first be salted and peppered. Fry quickly in boiling fat.

Pure, delicate, strong—Virot's Extracts.

Sauces.

BROWN SAUCE WITH MUSHROOMS.
Mrs. Barrett-Howard.

¼ pound of bacon.
1 tablespoonful of flour.
1 tablespoonful of Worcestershire sauce.
½ pint of stock.
1 tablespoonful of mushroom catsup.
1 tablespoonful of sherry.
Salt and pepper to taste.
1 cup of fresh or canned mushrooms, chopped.

Slice the bacon, put in a frying pan and try out all the fat. Take out the bacon, add flour and stir until smooth. Add the stock; stir continually till it boils. Then add the Worcestershire sauce, mushroom catsup, salt, pepper and the mushrooms. When mushrooms are thoroughly heated, take from the fire and add the wine. If the mushrooms are fresh, cook first in a little butter, stirring all the time.

SPANISH SAUCE FOR BOILED SALMON TROUT.
Mrs. MacDonald Moore.

Make a rich cream dressing. Boil and strain ¼ as much tomato as there is dressing. Add to cream dressing, the strained tomatoes; 3 hard boiled eggs, chopped fine; 1 teaspoonful of Worcestershire sauce; cayenne pepper and salt to taste.

Equaled by none—Virol's Extracts.

BEARNAISE SAUCE.

Mrs. Barrett-Howard.

Yolks of 4 eggs.
4 tablespoonfuls of olive oil.
¼ teaspoonful of salt.
4 tablespoonfuls of hot water.
1 tablespoonful of tarragon vinegar.
Cayenne to taste,

Beat the yolks till creamy; add the water and oil. Stand the bowl in a pan of boiling water, and stir till the eggs thicken. Take from the fire and add the vinegar, salt and pepper. Serve with broiled steak.

CREAM HORSERADISH SAUCE.

Mrs. Barrett-Howard.

1 bottle of grated horseradish, drained from the vinegar, and 1 pint of whipped cream. Add horseradish to cream gradually, stirring lightly just before serving.

SAUCE HOLLANDAISE.

Mrs. Barrett-Howard.

2 tablespoonfuls of butter.
1 tablespoonful of flour.
½ pint of boiling water.
½ teaspoonful of salt.
Yolks of 2 eggs.
Juice of ½ lemon.
1 teaspoonful of onion juice.
1 tablespoonful of chopped parsley.

Mix the butter and flour to a smooth paste in a bowl. Place the bowl over the fire in a pan of boiling water. Add the ½ pint of boiling water gradually, stiring until it thickens; add the salt. Take from the fire; add gradually the yolks of eggs (beaten); then add the juice of lemon, onion juice and parsley. Serve with fish.

For fastidious tastes—Virot's Extracts.

SAUCE TARTARE.
Mrs. C. M. Rathbun.

½ pint mayonnaise dressing.
3 olives.   1 gherkin.
1 tablespoonful of capers.

Chop olives, gherkin and capers very fine; add them to the dressing with 1 tablespoonful of tarragon vinegar, and it is ready to use. Serve with smelts, lobster, chops, etc.

MUSTARD DRESSING FOR COLD MEATS.
Mrs. G. M. Newton.

Boil an egg 20 or 30 minutes. When cold, remove the yolk; mash, and add to it 1 heaping teaspoonful Coleman's mustard, 1 even teaspoonful of salt, 2 teaspoonfuls of oil or melted butter. Do not add the oil or butter until the egg, mustard and salt are thoroughly mixed. Lastly add vinegar, or juice of a lemon, until of the right consistency.

TOMATO SAUCE.
Mrs. Barrett-Howard.

1 pint of stewed tomatoes.
1 tablespoonful of butter.
1 tablespoonful of flour.
1 small onion.
1 bay leaf.
1 sprig of parsley.
1 blade of mace.
Salt and pepper to taste.

Put the tomatoes on the fire, with the onion, bay leaf, parsley and mace, and simmer slowly for 10 minutes. Melt the butter; add to it the flour; mix until smooth. Press the tomatoes through a sieve; add them to the butter and flour. Stir continually until it boils; add salt and pepper.

For dainty toilets—Virot's Perfumes, Toilet Waters, Sachets.

Vegetables.

ASPARAGUS ON TOAST.
Mrs. C. M. Rathbun.

Wash the asparagus and cut off the tough ends. Soak in cold water ½ hour. Now tie it in small bundles and put into kettle of boiling water, and boil 20 minutes; add 1 teaspoonful of salt and boil 10 minutes longer. While the asparagus is cooking, boil 2 eggs hard. Toast squares of bread; butter while hot, and lay on a hot platter. Carefully drain the asparagus and lay it on toast, heads all one way. Put 1 tablespoonful of butter to melt, adding 1 tablespoonful of flour; mix until smooth; add ½ pint water in which asparagus was boiled; stir constantly until it boils. Season with salt and pepper to taste, and pour over the asparagus and sliced eggs. If liked, a little vinegar may be added to the sauce, and is a great improvement.

CORN OYSTERS.
Miss Thompson.

1 dozen ears of corn. Salt and pepper to taste.
1 tablespoonful of flour. 1 egg.

Score the corn down the center of each row of the grains; then with the back of a knife press out the pulp, leaving hull on the cob. Add the beaten egg, flour and seasoning. (If the corn is very juicy, you may have to add more flour; but you only want enough so as to be able to turn). Drop a spoonful on a griddle or in a well greased spider; brown on one side and then on the other.

Demand and Get—Virot's Perfumes and Extracts.

CORN FRITTERS.

Mrs. A. R. Maytum.

To 1 pint of sweet milk, add enough flour to make a stiff batter; 1 egg, 1 teaspoonful of baking powder in the flour; a pinch of salt. Add to this ½ can of canned corn. Drop in hot fat and fry until done.

SOUR BEANS.

Mrs. G. S. Josselyn.

String the beans and break into inch lengths. Pour over them as little hot water as will boil them, and cook until soft. (If young and tender, 20 minutes will cook them). Drain through a sieve, perfectly dry. Put into a sauce pan 1 tablespoonful of butter, 1 teaspoonful of flour, about 1 tablespoonful of vinegar, salt and pepper. Add the beans and let all cook together a few minutes. Just before taking up, beat up an egg light and add to it. Of course the dressing for the beans must be added to according to the amount of beans used.

FRIED EGG-PLANT.

Mrs. L. McKinstry.

Pare the egg-plant and cut into thin slices; sprinkle each slice with salt and pepper; pile them evenly on a deep plate; put a plate on top, and on this a heavy flat iron, to press out the juice. Let stand 1 hour. Beat 1 egg lightly, and add 1 tablespoonful of boiling water; dip each slice into this and then in bread crumbs. Put 3 tablespoonfuls lard or dripping into a frying pan; when hot, fry the slices brown on one side and then on the other. As the fat is consumed, add more, waiting each time for it to get hot before putting in the egg-plant. Drain on brown paper, and serve very hot with tomato catsup.

Price to suit all—Virot's Products.

KAL DOLMA—A SWEDISH DISH.
Emma Johnson.

Take 1 solid head of white cabbage. Boil until half done. Take up, and let drain until cold. Take beef or veal and chop until fine; season with pepper, salt, butter, cream, and a pinch of sugar; work all together until well mixed. Then take the cabbage, cut off the large leaves, taking out the hard stem, and in each leaf put a spoonful of the meat mixture. Shape into oblong rolls, folding the cabbage leaf all around, and lay carefully down in the kettle in which is enough cold water to cover; add butter and cover the kettle. Then boil slowly, basting often, and turn when brown on one side. Cook about 2 hours. Take up, and serve with brown gravy.

STEWED MUSHROOMS.
Miss Carrie Pratt.

Peel the mushrooms, wash in water and cut off the bottom of the stalk. Put in porcelain-lined kettle; to every pint of mushrooms, add 1 tablespoonful of butter. Divide butter into 2 balls, and roll in flour. Let mushrooms cook in their own liquor, with butter and flour, 15 minutes. Add salt and pepper and serve. Or 2 tablespoonfuls of cream can be added to the above; then take from fire and add beaten yolk of 1 egg and 1 tablespoonful of sherry. Serve immediately.

DELMONICO HASHED POTATOES.
Mrs. C. D. Armstrong.

Pare and chop 6 medium sized potatoes. It is best to cut them in moderately thick slices before chopping. When chopped put them into a baking-dish; season with salt and pepper; cover them with milk; place over the top 2 ounces of butter, cut into small bits. Bake in a quick oven 40 minutes.

Something modern—Virot's Extracts.

POTATO CROQUETTES.
Mrs. M. T. Dana.

3 coffee cups of mashed potatoes; ⅓ cup of milk; small tablespoonful of butter; yolks of 2 eggs. Parsley, onion juice, salt, red and black pepper to taste. Shape, roll in egg and crumbs, and fry in hot lard. It is best to prepare them some hours before frying.

SILVERTHORNE POTATOES.
Mrs. R. H. Barnum.

Remove the thin skin from baked potatoes. Put cream or milk, with some butter, salt and pepper in a double boiler. When boiling, add the potatoes chopped, and cook ¾ of an hour.

SWEET POTATO CROQUETTES.
Miss Pritchard.

Boil, peel and mash 4 good sized potatoes; add butter size of an egg, ½ teaspoonful of salt and a dash of cayenne; beat until smooth, form into cylinder-shaped croquettes. Dip in egg and then in bread crumbs, and fry in smoking hot fat.

OYSTER-PLANT FRITTERS.
Mrs. Rorer.

1 dozen roots; 1 tablespoonful of flour; 1 teaspoonful of salt; 1 saltspoonful pepper; 2 eggs, well beaten.

Scrape the oyster-plant or salsify, and as fast as you do so throw the pieces in cold water to prevent discoloration. When all are done, cut them into slices and boil 30 minutes. Drain and mash through a colander; add to the roots the flour, salt, pepper and eggs. Mix; form the mixture into oyster-shaped cakes. Fry in very hot Cottolene, on both sides.

Better than the Best—Virot's Extracts.

BAKED ONIONS.

Mrs. S. B. Durlin.

Boil onions until tender, but not soft. Place in the dish in which they are to be baked. Take a sharp knife and make a hole in the center of each, putting in a small piece of butter. Salt and pepper to taste. Sprinkle flour over the top, and cover with sweet milk. Bake 1 hour.

RICE CAKES.

Miss Lizzie Lester.

1 egg, white and yolk beaten separately; ½ cup of milk; ½ pint of flour; ½ teacup of cooked rice; 1 teaspoonful of baking powder. Fry in plenty of hot lard. A tablespoonful of batter for each cake.

RICE AND TOMATOES.

Mrs. M. L. Moore.

Boil 1 can of tomatoes, with 3 or 4 slices of bacon and 1 small onion, until thoroughly cooked. Season with salt, pepper, a little sugar and a good sized piece of butter; then add rice, previously boiled as follows: Thoroughly clean and wash 1 pound of rice; put into a kettle containing 1 gallon boiling water, well salted, stirring occasionally with a fork. Boil from 10 to 15 minutes; then drain through a colander and add to tomatoes, mixing thoroughly.

SCALLOPED TOMATOES.

Mrs. Kate Cushing.

Butter the baking dish. Put in a layer of cracker crumbs; then a layer of sliced or cooked tomatoes, which have been seasoned with salt, pepper, Virot's extract of onion and celery salt. Then another layer of cracker crumbs, tomatoes, etc., until the dish is filled. Bake ½ hour in a hot oven.

Pure, delicate, strong—Virot's Extracts.

STUFFED TOMATOES.

Mrs. A. R. Maytum.

Wash 6 medium sized tomatoes. Remove the stem and core. To 1 teacup of bread crumbs, add 1 small onion, chopped fine, chopped parsley; season to taste with pepper and salt, and wet with boiling water. Mix thoroughly. Stuff tomatoes as full as possible, and bake 30 minutes.

FRIED TOMATOES.

Mrs. C. M. Rathbun.

Cut ripe tomatoes in thick slices; dredge with flour. Put 2 tablespoonfuls of butter or drippings in pan; when hot lay tomatoes in, with flour side down. Fry on both sides. When done place on a hot platter. Remove any burnt pieces that may be in the pan. Add 1 tablespoonful of butter and 2 tablespoonfuls of flour; stir continually until brown, then add 1 pint of milk; cook until smooth; season and pour over tomatoes.

BAKED BEANS.

Mrs. J. C. Mullett.

1 quart of beans; ½ pound of salt pork. Place in cold water; boil 30 minutes. Drain; place again in cold water, and boil until tender. Add 2 tablespoonfuls of molasses, a little white pepper; also salt, if pork has not salted it sufficiently. Cut the rind of the pork into gashes 1 inch deep, place on the top of the beans; bake in a hot oven till brown. Or, cut the pork into thin bits, mix through the beans; bake in a covered dish 3 hours.

Equaled by none—Virot's Extracts.

Sundries.

SCRAMBLED EGGS.
Mrs. William White.

12 eggs. ½ cup of cream.
1 cup of chopped ham (boiled.) Butter enough to cover the bottom of the spider.

Beat the eggs until light. Have the spider hot, in which is the melted butter; pour in the eggs, stirring constantly. When they begin to thicken, add the cream and the chopped ham, and allow it to cook a minute or two, still stirring. Season with salt and pepper, according to taste. These eggs are very nice without the chopped ham.

FRENCH OMELET.
Mrs. S. G. Skinner.

1 cup of boiling milk.
1 cup of bread crumbs (fine and soft).
Butter size of an egg.
6 eggs, beaten separately.

Pour the boiling milk over the butter and crumbs. When cool add the yolks of eggs, beaten light. Just before frying, mix lightly the beaten whites of the eggs. Fry in butter. Season. This makes two omelets.

OMELET WITH SMOKED BEEF.
Mrs. M. H. Taylor.

Beat the yolks and whites of 6 eggs separately. Put 1 tablespoonful of butter into a frying-pan and cook in it for

For fastidious tastes—Virot's Extracts.

a couple of minutes, 2 tablespoonfuls of smoked beef. Mix the yolks and whites of eggs lightly together. Turn these into the pan upon the beef, and proceed as with a plain omelet.

DEVILLED EGGS.
Mrs. Pratt.

Boil 8 eggs hard. Mash the yolks fine; add 1 teaspoonful salt, ½ teaspoonful of dry mustard, large pinch of cayenne, 1 large tablespoonful of oil or 2 large tablespoonfuls melted butter, 3 tablespoonfuls weak vinegar, and 4 tablespoonfuls fine bread crumbs.

This is an old recipe. Perhaps "paprika" would be better than cayenne.

EGG SCALLOP.
Mrs. H. D. Jarvis.

6 eggs, boiled hard; the yolks mashed and the whites chopped fine. 1 pint, more or less, of cold boiled ham, chopped fine. Melt 1 tablespoonful of butter, add 2 tablespoonfuls of flour; rub together, and when smooth add gradually 1 pint of milk; boil until it thickens. Season with salt and cayenne. Place in alternate layers in a baker, the ham, whites and yolks of eggs and cream sauce, ending with the cream sauce on top. Sprinkle with buttered cracker crumbs, and place in the oven to brown.

FRENCH TOAST.

For 6 persons. Take 2 eggs, ½ cup of milk, and flour enough to make a thick batter. Cut old bread in thin slices. Dip in the batter, and fry in butter. Serve hot.

ESCALLOPED EGGS.

Melt a small piece of butter and 2 thin slices of cheese. Put in the number of eggs you wish to use. Put in different places over the eggs, small pieces of butter; season with

For dainty toilets—Virot's Perfumes, Toilet Waters, Sachets.

salt and pepper. Now sprinkle thickly over the top nice bread crumbs. Place in the oven and let remain until the yolks are of a jelly-like consistency, and serve.

CHEESE CROQUETTES.
Miss Heyl.

2 cups grated cheese.
1 cup of fine bread crumbs.
Salt and cayenne to taste.

Form into small balls; dip into beaten eggs and fine cracker crumbs. Fry in boiling fat. Serve with salads.

CHEESE STRAWS.
Mac Hayward.

1½ cups of flour; ½ cup of butter; 1 cup grated cheese; yolk of 1 egg; saltspoonful of salt; pinch of cayenne pepper; 2 tablespoonfuls of sweet milk. Cut in narrow strips, about 4 inches long and ¼ inch thick; bake a light brown.

CHEESE FONDU.
Mrs. MacDonald Moore.

Let 1 pint of sweet milk come to a boil. Put in it 1 tablespoonful of butter. Wet 2 tablespoonfuls sifted flour in a little cold milk, and stir into the boiling milk; with ½ pound of cheese cut fine, or better, run through meat grinder. When the cheese melts, set it off the stove. Season with salt and cayenne pepper to taste. Beat 4 eggs separately and stir with the cheese mixture. Put into a buttered pan and bake 20 minutes, allowing room to rise.

CHEESE SOUFFLE.
Mrs. Joseph Brown.

2 tablespoonfuls of butter. When melted, add 1 heaping tablespoonful of flour; stir until smooth and frothy, being careful not to brown. Gradually stir into this, 1 cup milk;

Demand and Get—Virot's Perfumes and Extracts.

let it boil up; then stir 1 heaping cup of grated cheese. Add a teaspoonful of salt and pinch of red pepper. Beat light the yolks of 3 eggs with a teaspoonful of water; stir throughly into the mixture. Pour into a bowl and set aside to cool. Beat whites of 3 eggs to stiff froth, and beat into cold mixture. Have basin buttered; pour in and bake from 20 to 30 minutes, and serve at once.

DELICIOUS SANDWICHES.
Mrs. Seldon E. Stone.

2 heads of crisp celery, chopped very fine. Set away to become very cold. Add ½ cup of grated cheese; ½ cup of cream, after being whipped stiff. Very good.

CELERY SANDWICHES.

Chop crisp stalks of celery very fine, and mix with it some mayonnaise dressing, and spread between the bread. These are particularfy appetizing for traveling lunches, as they keep moist so long.

ASPIC JELLY.
Mrs. Joseph Brown.

½ pint of clear stock. (Beef used for amber jelly; and chicken or veal, for white jelly).

½ box gelatine, soaked in ½ cup cold water for 2 hours.

White of 1 egg; 2 cloves; 1 large slice of onion; 12 pepper corns; 1 stalk celery; 1 small bay leaf.

Put the stock and other ingredients together on to boil. When it gets hot, beat the white of the egg with 1 spoonful of cold stock; stir in and let boil up. Set back where it will simmer 20 minutes. Strain through a napkin and turn into mould or shallow dish, and put away to harden.

Price to suit all—Virot's Products.

YORKSHIRE PUDDING.

Mrs. Lamira J. White.

When roast beef is done, or about 15 minutes before taking to the table, take the meat out, and divide the gravy; ½ to be thickened as usual, the richer half left in the dripping pan. Then take 1 pint of sweet milk; 2 eggs; 1 teaspoonful of salt; 1 teaspoonful of baking powder, stirred into the flour. Use flour enough to make a batter like pan-cakes. Pour this into the dripping-pan, over the gravy, and bake 15 or 20 minutes. When done, roll up and serve on the same platter with the meat, and cut in slices.

To be served with roast beef.

Breads, Rolls, Gems, Etc.

RECIPES.

In many of the following recipes, COTTOLENE is used for shortening and frying. COTTOLENE is made of 80 per cent. tripple refined Cottonseed Oil and 20 per cent. of choice beef suet, assuring users the purest possible shortening and frying fat, palatable and digestible. It can be used for many purposes in the place of butter and when it is impossible to use lard.

For the benefit of the uninitiated, we give the following directions for using this delectable product :

In using COTTOLENE for shortening, all rules for lard or butter hold good, except in quantity—one-third less of COTTOLENE being required. This must be strictly observed, or the food will be too rich.

In frying, use the same amount of COTTOLENE as you would of lard, but care must be exercised in heating. Always put it on in a cold vessel—COTTOLENE heats without sputtering or smoking and quicker than lard, with the same heat. Never allow it to smoke, as it is then burning. COTTOLENE should be tested according to the nature of the food to be fried, viz.: for croquettes, fish-balls, oysters, etc., drop a small piece of bread in the hot fat. If it browns quickly on coming to the top, the fat is hot enough. Doughnuts, potatoes, fritters, etc., require slightly lower temperature, as they must be cooked through while browning. Test the fat for these by dropping in a piece of dough. If it rises to the top and browns in one minute, the fat is hot enough.

Better than the Best—Virot's Extracts.

RUSKS.

Mrs. F. L. Gillette.

2 cups raised dough; 1 cup sugar; ⅓ cup COTTOLENE; 2 well beaten eggs; flour.

SALLY LUNN.

Mrs. F. L. Gillette.

⅓ cup of COTTOLENE; 1 pint of milk; 4 eggs; 1 tablespoonful of sugar; 1 teaspoonful of salt; ½ cup of yeast, or ⅓ cake of compressed yeast; 7 cups sifted flour.

Scald the milk; when cold add COTTOLENE, sugar, salt and yeast. Beat thoroughly, and set it to rise over night. In the morning dissolve the soda in a spoonful of water, stir it in the batter with the well-beaten eggs. Turn all into a well-greased cake dish to rise again. Bake about 45 minutes, and serve warm from the oven.

POP-OVERS.

Mrs. F. L. Gillette.

2 cups of milk; 2 cups of flour; 1 teaspoonful of salt; 3 eggs; 1 small teaspoonful of melted COTTOLENE.

Beat the eggs until very light, then add to them the milk and salt. Add this little by little to the flour to prevent its being lumpy. Strain it through a sieve, filll well-greased gem-pans ½ full. Bake in a quick oven about 25 minutes.

MINUTE BISCUIT.

Marion Harland.

1 pint of sour or buttermilk; 1 teaspoonful of soda; 1⅓ teaspoonfuls of COTTOLENE; flour to make soft dough.

Have dough just stiff enough to handle; mix, roll and cut out rapidly, with as little handling as possible, and bake in a quick oven.

Pure, delicate, strong—Virot's Extracts.

BUTTER CRACKERS.
Marion Harland.

1 quart of flour; 2 tablespoonfuls of COTTOLENE; ½ teaspoonful soda, dissolved in hot water; 1 saltspoonful salt; 2 cups of sweet milk.

Rub the COTTOLENE into the flour, or, what is better, cut it up with a knife or chopper, as you do in pastry; add the salt, milk and soda, mixing well. Work into a ball, turning and shifting the mass often. Roll into an even sheet ¼ of an inch thick, or less, prick deeply with a fork, and bake in a moderate oven. Hang them up in a muslin bag in the kitchen for two days to dry.

GRAHAM WAFERS.
Mrs. Lincoln.

⅓ cup of Cottolene; ⅓ cup of sugar; ½ teaspoonful of salt; 1 pint of white flour; 1 pint of Graham flour.

Mix the Cottolene with the sugar and salt. Rub the mixture into the white and Graham flour mixed. Wet it with cold water into a very stiff dough. Knead it well, and roll out very thin. Cut in squares and bake quickly.

ROLLS.
Mrs. S. G. Skinner.

To 1 pint of new milk, take lard the size of an egg; let this boil. When cool, add 1 tablespoonful of sugar, 1 teaspoonful of salt, and the whites of two eggs, beaten stiff, ½ of a yeast cake, and flour to make a batter. Set this in a warm place to rise. When light make into a loaf and knead 10 minutes. Let this rise, then make into rolls; rub top over with melted butter, and when light bake in a quick oven about 25 minutes.

PARKER HOUSE ROLLS.
Mrs. Kirkover.

Take 1 quart of sifted flour; 1 quart of milk; 1 large tablespoonful of lard (not melted); mix to soft sponge. Add

Equaled by none—Virot's Extracts.

1 tablespoonful of sugar and 1 tablespoonful of salt. Let sponge rise 2 hours. Add 1 tablespoonful of butter and about 1 quart of flour and knead 15 minutes; put back in the pan and let rise again 2 hours. Put on a bread board, roll out and cut with small round cutter; spread with melted butter; fold them over and put in tins for baking, and let rise again about ½ hour. Bake in quick oven 15 or 20 minutes.

BAKING POWDER BISCUIT.

Miss Emma Thompson.

1 quart of sifted flour.
1 teaspoonful of salt.
2 heaping teaspoonfuls of baking powder.
1 large tablespoonful shortening (½ lard and ½ butter).
About 1 cup of milk—enough to make a soft dough.

Mix very quickly, put on a board, roll out and cut with cutter. Bake in a very quick oven.

RUSK.

Mrs. A. S. Couch.

1 pint of milk.
3 cups of flour.
½ cup of butter.
1 small cup of sugar.
3 eggs.
½ teaspoonful of salt.
½ yeast cake.

Scald milk and melt the butter in it. When luke-warm add yolks of eggs, salt and yeast, dissolved in ½ cup of water. When light add the sugar, whites of eggs and flour enough to mould. Let it rise again very light, then cut into small cakes. Bake quickly. Rub the tops with cream and sugar.

For fastidious tastes—Virot's Extracts.

CINNAMON BUNS.

Mrs. C. M. Rathbun.

Scald ½ pint of milk; add piece of butter size of an egg; 2 eggs, well beaten; add yeast cake, dissolved in about 2 tablespoonfuls of warm water, and sufficient flour to make a soft dough. Knead lightly and stand away till it doubles its bulk. When very light roll out, spread with butter, dust thickly with sugar and lightly with cinnamon and currants. Roll, cut into buns, stand in a greased pan and then in a warm place for about 1 hour. Bake in moderate oven.

POP-OVERS.

Mrs. A. S. Fox.

Beat 2 eggs, without separating; add to them ½ pint of milk. Pour this carefully, stirring all the while, into ½ pint of sifted flour. Strain at once into greased hot gem pans, and bake in a moderately quick oven at least 35 minutes. If not sufficiently baked they will fall when taken from the oven.

RYE PUFFS.

Mrs. J. C. Frisbee.

Beat together 1 tablespoonful of sugar, and 1 egg; add 1 cupful of milk, 1 cupful of rye flour, and ½ cupful of wheat flour in which is 1 teaspoonful of baking powder. Beat hard and bake in a quick oven.

MUFFINS.

1 pint of flour, 1 teaspoonful of baking powder and a little salt sifted together. Add to the beaten yolks of 2 eggs, 1 teacupful of sweet milk or cream, a piece of butter size of an egg. Melt the butter and stir all together well, and lastly add the whites of the 2 eggs, well beaten. Bake quickly in a hot oven and serve immediately.

For dainty toilets—Virot's Perfumes, Toilet Waters, Sachets.

CORN MUFFINS.

Mrs. Kingsland.

2 cups of sour milk; 2 tablespoonfuls of brown sugar; a little salt; 1 teaspoonful of soda; ½ cup of flour; and corn meal enough to make it moderately stiff. Bake in gem-tins for 20 minutes in a hot oven.

POTATO MUFFINS.

Mrs. S. G. Skinner.

3 medium sized potatoes, boiled and mashed fine. Add salt, 1 tablespoonful of sugar, 1 large tablespoonful of lard, 1 cup of milk, 1 egg well beaten, ½ yeast cake, dissolved in the milk. Stir in flour enough to make a stiff dough, and set in a warm place—at 12 o'clock, if wanted for tea. At 4 o'clock mix in more flour, roll out and cut with a cake cutter; set to rise again. At 6 o'clock they should be light. Bake 10 minutes in a hot oven.

GRAHAM GEMS.

Mrs. Kingsland.

1 pint of milk; 1 egg; a little salt; 2 tablespoonfuls of sugar; 1 teaspoonful of baking powder, stirred in a little flour; and Graham flour to make just stiff enough to drop from a spoon nicely. Have oven quite hot. Bake 20 minutes.

GRAHAM GEMS.

Mrs. George Wiley.

2 tablespoonfuls of sugar; 1 cup of sour milk; 1 cup of Graham flour; ½ cup wheat flour; 1 egg; 2 tablespoonfuls melted shortening; 1 teaspoonful of soda; a pinch of salt.

Sweet milk and 1 teaspoonful of baking powder may be substituted for sour milk and soda.

Demand and Get—Virot's Perfumes and Extracts.

INDIAN MEAL GEMS.

Mrs. Joseph Brown.

2 eggs; 2 tablespoonfuls melted butter; 2 tablespoonfuls granulated sugar; 2 cups sweet milk; 1 cup Indian meal; 1½ cups flour; 3 teaspoonfuls baking powder.

Beat the eggs thoroughly; add butter, sugar and milk, then meal, flour and baking powder. Bake in buttered gem-pans about 20 minutes.

WAFFLES.

Mrs. E. D. Clark.

1 pint of milk; 3½ cups of flour; 4 teaspoonfuls of sugar; 1 tablespoonful melted lard; 1 tablespoonful melted butter; a little salt; ½ cake of compressed yeast, dissolved in cold water.

Let the batter rise over night. In the morning add 2 eggs, 1 teaspoonful of baking powder. Bake in waffle irons, heated and well greased.

WAFFLES.

Mrs. M. M. Fenner.

3 eggs; 1 quart of sour milk; 1 teaspoonful soda; a little salt; 3 tablespoonfuls melted butter.

Beat the yolks thoroughly, stir in the melted butter and soda, and lastly the whites beaten stiff. Use flour to make stiffer than for pan-cakes. Bake in waffle iron.

1 quart sweet milk and 2 teaspoonfuls of baking powder can be substituted for the sour milk and soda.

WHEAT GRIDDLE CAKES.

Mrs. S. G. Skinner.

1 pint of sour milk; 1 egg; a little salt; 1 tablespoonful melted butter; flour to make batter the right consistency.

Beat this until very smooth, and when ready to bake put in sufficient soda to sweeten the milk. Bake a trial cake to see if right.

Price to suit all—Virot's Products.

RICE GRIDDLE CAKES.
Clara Anderson.

1 cup cold boiled rice; 1 quart of sour milk; 1 teaspoonful soda; 1 teaspoonful salt; 1 egg; a little butter, melted; and flour enough to make a batter.

INDIAN MEAL GRIDDLE CAKES.
Mrs. Joseph Brown.

1 egg; 1 cup of sour milk; ½ cup of meal; ¼ cup flour; 1 teaspoonful of soda; 1 teaspoonful of salt.

Beat the eggs light, add the salt, milk, meal and flour, and the soda, dissolved in a very little hot water.

FLANNEL CAKES.
Mrs. Lamira J. White.

1 pint of fresh buttermilk; 1 teaspoonful of soda; 5 eggs beaten separately, putting yolks into the batter; salt; and flour enough to make quite a stiff batter.

Then beat the whites of the eggs to a stiff froth; lay in the pan with the batter. Dip on the griddle first a small spoonful of the batter then some of the beaten whites, then cover over with the batter. Bake a light brown and turn. Serve with melted butter poured over.

BUCKWHEAT CAKES.
Mrs. L. R. White.

1 large cup sifted Graham flour; 2 cups buckwheat flour; 1 large spoonful of molasses; 1 small spoonful of salt; ⅔ cup of liquid hop yeast; water or milk to make right consistency to bake. Before baking in the morning, add 1 teaspoonful of soda, dissolved in a little water. When you add to this for next day, keep your proportions the same of everything, and once a week add new yeast.

Something modern—Virci's Extracts.

JOHNNY CAKE.
Mrs. Palmer.

1 cup meal; 1 cup flour; 2 tablespoonfuls of sugar; 1 egg; 2 teaspoonfuls of baking powder; nearly ⅓ cup of melted butter; pinch of salt, and milk enough to make as thick as cake batter.

JOHNNY CAKE.
Mrs. J. A. Pemberton.

2 cups corn meal; 1 cup flour; 1 egg; butter half the size of egg; 2 tablespoonfuls of sugar; 1 pint of sour milk, or buttermilk; 1 teaspoonful of soda.

CORN PONE.
Mrs. Kate L. Cushing.

Take 12 ears of cold boiled corn, grate it; mix with 1 quart of milk, lump of butter size of an egg, salt and pepper to taste, 2 eggs well beaten. Bake ¾ of an hour.

YEAST.
Mrs. George Manton.

12 good sized potatoes; 3 tablespoonfuls sugar; 3 tablespoonfuls flour; 2 tablespoonfuls salt; 2 compressed yeast cakes.

Mash potatoes; mix flour, salt and sugar to a smooth paste with boiling water; add this to the potatoes. Thin; put in 6 pints of hot water; when luke-warm add yeast cakes. Let rise over night.

BREAD.

Take 1 pint of this yeast for a loaf of bread. Warm to blood heat; add 1 tablespoonful melted lard; mix into hard loaf. Put into baking tin; let rise once and bake.

Keep yeast in cool place in open fruit cans. This will make about 8 loaves of bread.

Better than the Best—Virot's Extracts.

BREAD.
Mrs. A. B. Cobb.

Take 6 boiled potatoes, mash fine and pour on them 1 quart of water. Take 1 tablespoonful of salt; 2 tablespoonfuls sugar; 3 tablespoonfuls of flour. Scald with 1 pint of boiling water and add to potatoes; then add ½ cake of yeast, dissolved. Set in a warm place until light, then keep in a cool place. This is a sufficient quantity for 6 loaves, and will keep for several days in glass cans.

When ready to bake, allow a large cup of yeast for a loaf of bread. Use no other wetting. Knead with flour and a little lard for 20 minutes. Put in tins, let rise and bake.

WHOLE WHEAT BREAD.
Mrs. C. M. Rathbun.

Pour 1 pint of boiling water into 1 pint sweet milk. When luke-warm add 1 teaspoonful of salt and 1 compressed yeast cake, dissolved in 2 tablespoonfuls of warm water. Mix and stir in sufficient whole wheat flour to make a batter that will drop from a spoon. Beat well. Cover and stand in a warm place (75 degrees Fahr.) for 3 hours, until very light. Then stir in more flour, enough to make a soft dough. Knead lightly until the greater part of the stickiness is lost. Now mould it into 3 or 4 loaves, according to the size of your pans; place in greased pans, cover and stand aside again in a warm place for an hour. Bake in a moderately quick oven 35 or 40 minutes.

This whole wheat bread cannot be made stiff like the ordinary white bread, so must be handled quickly and lightly on the board. Always select flour that is free from outside bran.

MY MOTHER'S RYE BREAD.
Mrs. M. M. Fenner.

Take rye flour, and make sponge same as you would for wheat bread. In the sponge put ¼ cup of molasses or

Pure, delicate, strong—Virot's Extracts.

sugar (molasses makes it darker). When this sponge has risen light enough, knead until it won't take any more flour; it will take more than other bread. because it is so sticky. Put in a warm place to rise, which will take a little longer than for other bread. Then make into loaves and let rise again. When light put in a hot oven and bake about ¾ of an hour.

GRAHAM BREAD.
Mrs. Esther Cushing.

2½ cups of sour milk; 1 cup of molasses; 2 teaspoonfuls of soda; 1 teaspoonful salt; 4 cups of Graham flour. Let rise 2 hours. Bake ¾ of an hour.

GRAHAM BREAD.
Mrs. George G. Miner.

1 cup of molasses; ½ cup of sugar; 2 cups of sour milk; 1 teaspoonful of soda; 1 teaspoonful of baking powder; 2 cups of Graham flour, and enough wheat flour to thicken like gems; salt. Bake in a moderate oven.

INDIAN LOAF.
Miss Lizzie Lester.

1 quart of sour milk.
1 quart of Indian meal.
1 pint of flour.
½ cup of molasses.
1 teaspoonful of salt.
1 teaspoonful of soda.

Put in a round tin or tin pail, set in a pail of boiling water and boil 3 hours.

BROWN BREAD.
Mrs. S. J. Gifford.

For 3 loaves.

½ of a yeast foam cake, dissolved in a little water; 1 cup of milk; 1½ cups of hot water; 1 small cup of molasses;

Equaled by none—Virot's Extracts.

2 tablespoonfuls of sugar; a little salt. Pour the hot water into the bowl upon the lard, the size of an egg. Mix all this together and add flour enough to make it stiff to stir with a spoon. Put into tins, stand in a warm place until light and bake over 1 hour in a moderate oven.

STEAMED BROWN BREAD.
Mrs. D. R. Manley.

2 cups of sweet milk.
2 cups of corn meal.
1½ cups of flour.
1 cup of New Orleans molasses.
1 teaspoonful of soda.
1 teapoonful of salt.
Steam 2½ hours, then dry in the oven for a short time.

For fastidious tastes—Virot's Extracts.

Salads.

MAYONNAISE DRESSING.
Mrs. MacDonald Moore.

3 eggs; ¼ teaspoonful salt; the juice of ½ lemon; and a most liberal sprinkling of cayenne pepper.

Stir oil into yolks very slowly until they begin to thicken, when it may be added more rapidly. Add the salt shortly, and then the lemon juice. Have everything very cold.

SALAD DRESSING.
Mae Hayward.

Yolks of 3 eggs; 3 tablespoonfuls of vinegar (1 of Tarragon); ½ teaspoonful of salt; ½ teaspoonful mustard.

Cook in double boiler until thick and creamy, stirring continually. When cold, add 3 large tablespoonfuls of salad oil, stirring slowly all the time. Just before serving, add 1 cup of whipped cream.

SALAD DRESSING.
Mrs. Festus Day.

The yolks of 2 well beaten eggs; 1 teaspoonful each of sugar and salt; ½ teaspoonful pepper; and 1½ teaspoonfuls of mustard; mix well.

Heat to the boiling point 1 cupful of vinegar and a lump of butter the size of a pigeon's egg. While this is heating, beat to a stiff froth the whites of the 2 eggs and mix with the other other ingredients, beating well; then add the

---

For dainty toilets—Virot's Perfumes, Toilet Waters, Sachets.

boiling vinegar, a few drops at a time. Set on the fire 2 or 3 minutes, stirring constantly; beat a few minutes after removing from the fire and set away to cool. When ready to use, mix with thick sweet cream.

SALAD DRESSING.
Mrs. Seldon E. Stone.

Boil the yolks of 3 eggs hard; put through a fine sieve; add slowly the yolks of 2 raw eggs; stir together until smooth. Add very slowly the oil; season with red pepper and salt, a little vinegar and a little lemon juice.

This is a fine dressing, and will keep a number of days.

CREAM DRESSING.

Heat ½ cup cream. Moisten 1 tablespoonful of cornstarch in a little milk; add it to the hot cream. Cook a moment, then stir in the well-beaten yolks of 2 eggs. Take from the fire, add ½ teaspoonful of salt, a dash of pepper, and 1 tablespoonful of vinegar or lemon juice.

FRENCH DRESSING.

1 tablespoonful of vinegar; ½ teaspoonful of salt; 3 tablespoonfuls of olive oil; ¼ teaspoonful black pepper.

Add salt and pepper to the oil and stir until dissolved, then add gradually the vinegar. Stir a minute and it is ready to use.

POTATO SALAD.
Mrs. Ward Barnum.

Slice boiled potatoes, and while hot pour over them sufficient French dressing, to which 1 teaspoonful of onion juice has been added. Let stand until perfectly cold. Bacon fried crisp and cut fine and added just before serving, improves the flavor.

Demand and Get—Virot's Perfumes and Extracts.

CELERY SALADS.
Mrs. Barrett-Howard.

I. Cut celery in small pieces and put in tomato jelly. Pour in small round moulds and let harden. Serve on lettuce with a circle of mayonnaise dressing around each mould. Use Tarragon vinegar in dressing.

II. A few peas and beets cut in small pieces, added to celery, cut as above, is delicious. Sprinkle vegetables with salt and pepper, and mix with mayonnaise. Serve on lettuce.

III. Cut celery, season with salt and pepper; mix with mayonnaise and serve on lettuce.

POTATO SALAD.
Mrs. G. S. Josselyn.

Boil 1 dozen fair sized potatoes with the skins on. Peel, cool and slice. 2 eggs, boiled hard; chop whites fine, and rub yolks into a bowl through a fine sieve. Chop a small onion fine and add to the whites of eggs. To the yolks add gradually 4 tablespoonfuls of salad oil. Pepper and salt, and 2 tablespoonfuls of vinegar. Put the sliced potatoes in a salad bowl and with a silver fork mix the whites of eggs and onions through, then pour the dressing over and mix thoroughly. Add more seasoning, if necessary.

VEAL SALAD AND DRESSING.
Miss Matilda Denton.

1 teacup of strong vinegar; a piece of butter the size of a hickory-nut and 1 tablespoonful of sugar. Put on the fire, and when hot add the beaten yolks of 6 eggs. Stir all the time till it thickens. Take from the fire and add the oil (or cream), salt and pepper to taste. Put celery salt on the veal. Pick up the veal, and add as much chopped cabbage as meat.

Price to suit all—Virot's Products.

TOMATO JELLY—MAYONNAISE DRESSING.

Mrs. G. S. Josselyn.

Heat and strain through a coarse sieve 1 can of tomatoes, removing all seeds. Add to the juice a generous seasoning of salt and white pepper. Dissolve ½ box of Cox's gelatine. When the gelatine is dissolved, and the tomato juice hot, mix both thoroughly together. Pour into a plain mould and place on ice. When set, turn on a platter and serve by cutting thin slices, each placed on a lettuce leaf, and cover with mayonnaise dressing.

CHICKEN SALAD.

Mrs. Jacobi.

Take a young, tender chicken of 2½ pounds. Boil for 1 hour, or should it be a fowl, boil ¾ or 1 hour longer. Season while boiling with a little salt; when cooked, let it get thoroughly cold. Bone the chicken and cut into small pieces, put in a deep dish; season with a pinch of salt, a little pepper, 1 tablespoonful of vinegar, or the juice of 1 large lemon, 3 leaves of chopped lettuce, and a few pieces of white celery cut small. Mix well; place it in a salad bowl and cover with ½ cupful of mayonnaise dressing. Decorate the top with a chopped hard boiled egg, a tablespoonful of capers, 12 stoned olives, quarters of 2 hard boiled eggs and 6 small lettuce leaves around dish, then serve. Very fine.

SWEETBREAD SALAD.

Mrs. C. M. Rathbun.

Soak 1 pair of sweetbreads in cold water 1 hour. Remove with a *silver* knife all fat and skin. Put sweetbreads in a *granite* sauce pan, cover with boiling water, and add 1 teaspoonful of salt and simmer 20 minutes. When done,

Something modern—Virot's Extracts.

put in cold water for five minutes. When cold, cut in thin slices. Rub a bowl with onion and make in it ½ pint of mayonnaise dressing (Tarragon vinegar added to dressing is a great improvement). Put a thin slice of onion in center of salad bowl and arrange lettuce leaves around it. Mix the sweetbreads with the dressing and put in center of dish.

SWEETBREAD SALAD WITH CUCUMBERS.

Mrs. MacDonald Moore.

1 pair of sweetbreads, parboiled and shredded in small pieces; an equal quantity of chopped cucumbers. Cover with French dressing; let stand 10 minutes on ice. Drain carfully and serve on lettuce with mayonnaise dressing.

TONGUE SALAD.

Miss Belle White.

1 tongue, boiled and chopped fine; ⅓ as much celery as tongue when they are chopped; 1 lemon, chopped, adding juice; 2 hard boiled eggs, sliced.

DRESSING.

2 tablespoonfuls of mustard, mixed with 1 tablespoonful of oil; 1 raw egg; salt and ¼ teaspoonful of red pepper; dressing poured over all.

ORANGE SALAD.

Mrs. M. M. Fenner.

Pare and pick up in pieces nice juicy oranges; pour over a little French dressing. Then place on the tender inside leaves of head lettuce, put on a spoonful of mayonnaise dressing and serve.

Better than the Best—Virot's Extracts.

WALDORF SALAD.

Miss Grace McKinstry.

Pare, core and cut into dice 4 large *sour* apples; add to them 1 quart of celery, cut into ½ inch pieces. Dust over them 1 teaspoonful of salt, 1 teaspoonful of paprika, and then 2 tablespoonfuls of Tarragon vinegar. Mix all together, then stir in 1½ cups of good stiff mayonnaise dressing.

PEANUT SALAD.

Miss Pratt.

Soak 1 cup of peanut meats in olive oil for 1½ hours. Drain and toss in salad bowl, with 2 cups of finely cut celery and 10 or 12 pitted olives. Mix with mayonnaise dressing.

Delicious to serve with duck.

Pies.

CURRANT PIE.
Mrs. Robert Jones.

1 cup of ripe currants, mashed; 1 cup of sugar; 1 heaping tablespoonful of flour; 2 tablespoonfuls of water; yolks of 2 eggs; use the whites of the eggs for frosting; 1 crust.

SNOW PIE.
Mrs. N. G. Richmond.

Make a smooth paste of 2 tablespoonfuls of cornstarch and 3 tablespoonfuls of cold water. Then pour in this paste 1 pint of boiling water and 1 cup of sugar. Boil well; add the white of 1 egg, beaten to a froth, and a pinch of salt. Add whipped white of 1 egg, into which has been stirred 1 tablespoonful of sugar. Spread on top and put in oven to brown. Flavor pie to taste, with Virot's flavoring.

LEMON PIE.
Mrs. C. A. Clute.

1 cup of sugar.
1 coffeecup of water.
1 heaping tablespoonful of cornstarch.
Juice and rind of 1 lemon.
1 tablespoonful of butter.
Yolks of 2 eggs.
Mix sugar, cornstarch and eggs together, adding a little

Equaled by none—Virot's Extracts.

cold water if necessary. Boil water with butter and juice and grated rind of the lemon. Add the sugar, cornstarch and eggs and cook until it thickens. Line pie tin with rich pastry and bake. Fill with the mixture. Beat the whites of 2 eggs with 2 tablespoonfuls of powdered sugar, and put in oven to brown.

PINEAPPLE CUSTARD.

Mrs. MacDonald Moore.

½ pound of butter.
2 cups of sugar.
5 eggs.
1 can of pineapple.

Cream butter with sugar; add the eggs, beaten separately and *very* light; then the chopped pineapple. The pastry must be put in tins and dried a little in stove before putting in the mixture. Cocoanut or lemons may be used instead of pineapple.

BANBERRY TARTS.

Mae Hayward.

1 pound raisins; ¼ pound of citron; 4 figs, chopped fine; juice and grated rind of 1 lemon; 1 cup of sugar; 3 rolled crackers; 3 tablespoonfuls of water.

Just heat through, but do not cook. When cool add 3 tablespoonfuls of brandy. This makes about 3 dozen. Cut good pastry with round cutter, and add 1 tablespoonful of the filling.

APPLE TART.

Mrs. C. M. Rathbun.

Fill pie plate with sliced apple; add sugar to taste, bits of butter and water enough to cook the apples. Then cover with a good plain paste.

For fastidious tastes—Virot's Extracts.

When ready to serve turn crust on to plate, spread apples and grate nutmeg on top. Serve with cream.

CREAM PIE-PLANT PIE.
Mrs. Wm. Parks.

1 cup cream; 1 cup sugar; 1 tablespoonful of flour; and enough pie-plant to cover bottom of dish.

Cut up pie-plant, and add ¼ teaspoonful of soda and pour on boiling water. Let stand on range a few minutes; then drain, and put in the bottom of a well-lined pie plate. Then add cream, then sugar, and lastly the flour. Cut top crust a little larger than the bottom of pie plate, and place over top, without pinching down.

MAPLE CUSTARD PIE.
Mrs. Barrett-Howard.

1 pint of cream or milk.
Yolks of 3 eggs.
1 cup of new maple sugar.
Pinch of salt.

Beat the sugar and eggs together; add the cream or milk. Line pie plate with good rough paste. Fill with the mixture and bake in a quick oven.

ORANGE TARTS.
Mrs. S. H. Quinby.

Line gem pans with good pastry. Bake and fill with a spoonful of Orange Marmalade or Conserve. Cover with meringue, made of the whites of eggs and 1 tablespoonful of powdered sugar to each egg.

Put in oven until light brown. Raspberry or other jams can be substituted for the Marmalade.

For dainty toilets—Virot's Perfumes, Toilet Waters, Sachets.

ENGLISH MINCE MEAT.

Miss Matilda Denton.

4 pounds of beef suet.
2 pounds of currants.
2 pounds of small raisins.
6 pounds of apples.
2½ pounds of brown sugar.
½ pound of candied orange peel.
½ pound of citron.
1 large nutmeg.
Rind of 2 lemons, chopped fine. and the juice of 1 lemon.
½ pint of brandy.
1 pound of English walnuts, chopped.

Wash and dry currants; seed raisins, chop them, and also the suet, fine; slice citron and orange peel very fine; grate nutmeg; pare and core the apples and chop fine; strain the lemon juice. Mix all well together, adding the brandy. Place the mixture in a jar, carefully excluding the air, and it will be ready for use in a few days.

Puddings.

PLUM PUDDING.

*Mrs. Thos. P. Dods, The Manse,
Wark-on-Tyne, England.*

4 ounces stoned raisins.
4 ounces sultana raisins.
4 ounces currants.
4 ounces minced apples.
6 ounces minced beef suet.
3 ounces flour.
3 ounces bread crumbs.
2 ounces lemon, orange and citron peel, mixed.
Season to taste with ground cloves, ginger and nutmeg.
Add a wine-glass (2 fl. oz.) of brandy, a very little milk and 4 eggs. Mix *very thoroughly*; butter a mould, fill it and cover with a paper or cloth, and steam 4 hours. Serve with arrow-root sauce, made with water and seasoned with brandy and a little sweet wine.

GRAHAM PUDDING.

Miss Stewart.

1 cup of molasses.
1 even teaspoonful of soda.
1 cup sweet milk.
2 cups Graham flour.
1 cup of seeded raisins, dredged with flour.
Steam 3 hours. Serve with hot wine sauce or with cream and sugar.

Price to suit all—Virot's Products.

SUET PUDDING.

Miss Ama L. Lester.

2 cups of chopped bread.
½ cup of chopped suet.
½ cup of molasses.
1 egg. 1 cup of raisins. 1 cup of sweet milk.
½ teaspoonful of soda, dissolved in milk.
½ teaspoonful of cloves. 1 teaspoonful of cinnamon.
Pinch of mace. Pinch of salt.
Boil 2 hours in the boiler. Serve with Foamy sauce.

FOAMY SAUCE.

Beat 1 cup of butter to a cream; add 1 cup of granulated sugar. Stir until white and foamy. Just before serving, pour into it 1 cup of boiling water and stir a moment.

STRAWBERRY DUMPLINGS.

Mrs. Louis McKinstry.

Put 1 pint of sifted flour into a bowl. Rub into it piece of butter size of an egg; add 1 teaspoonful of salt; 1 heaping teaspoonful of baking powder, and sufficient milk to moisten —about ½ cup. Mix quickly; take out and roll into a sheet ¼ of an inch thick; cut into cakes with a round biscuit cutter. Put about 3 strawberries into each cake, fold them over neatly and steam 20 minutes. Serve with Strawberry sauce.

STRAWBERRY SAUCE.

Beat butter size of an egg to a cream, adding gradually ½ cup of granulated sugar; then add 12 berries (1 at a time) mashing and beating until the whole is perfectly light. If it has a curdled appearance, add more sugar, and stand in a cool place until wanted.

Something modern—Virot's Extracts.

STEAMED CUP PUDDING.

Mrs. M. M. Fenner.

1 pint of sifted flour.
1 heaping teaspoonful of baking powder.
½ teaspoonful of salt.
1 teacup of sweet milk.

Butter 6 cups and fill ⅓ full, first putting in fruit—anything you like (canned cherries, blackberries or peaches). Steam 40 minutes. Serve with whipped cream or boiled sauce.

CHOCOLATE PUDDING.

Mrs. C. A. Clute.

1 quart of milk; heat over water; when boiling add ½ cup of grated chocolate.

Put into a bowl the following: 2 eggs, ½ cup of sugar, 2 tablespoonfuls cornstarch, 1 teaspoonful of Virot's Vanilla and a pinch of salt. Beat together, add to boiling milk and stir till it thickens. Pour into mould and set in cool place to harden. Serve with sweetened cream flavored with Virot's Extract of Vanilla.

STEAMED CHOCOLATE PUDDING.

Mrs. N. G. Richmond.

1 egg; ¾ cup of sugar; ½ cup of milk; 1½ cup of flour; 1 tablespoonful of melted butter; 2 squares of chocolate; 1½ teaspoonfuls of baking powder.

Steam 2 hours. Serve cool, with plenty of whipped cream, sweetened and stiffened with white of egg.

HEALTHFUL DESSERT.

Miss Jennie Prescott.

Have 1 quart of new milk. Into this stir a very small cup of cracked wheat and 1 cup of stoned raisins. Mix

Better than the Best—Virot's Extracts.

thoroughly and set it in a moderately hot oven to bake 2 hours, slowly at first, then faster. Stir every 10 minutes, so it will not brown. Let it cool, and eat with cream.

It should be thin when it comes from the oven, as it jellies when cold.

CREAM CUSTARD.

*Mrs. Thos. P. Dods, The Manse,
Wark-on-Tyne, England.*

1 breakfast cupful good cream (about 6 fl. oz).
The whites of 3 eggs.
1 tablespoonful of pounded loaf sugar.

Whip the eggs and sugar until they are a stiff, high froth. Bring the cream to a boil; draw it off the fire and stir in the egg quickly; then let it (the whole) just begin to boil and turn it into a bowl, stirring lightly a time or two. When cold pour into a glass dish; season with Virot's Lemon or Vanilla Extract.

FRENCH CUSTARD.

Mrs. R. H. Barnum.

3 eggs, beaten as for sponge cake.
¼ pound of sugar.
1 pint of whipped cream.

Flavor with brandy or wine, and serve in cups, with nutmeg on top.

MOUNTAIN-DEW PUDDING.

Miss Nellie C. Lake.

1 pint of milk.
Yolks of 2 eggs.
2 tablespoonfuls cocoanut.
½ cup of cracker crumbs.
½ cup sugar.
Bake half an hour. Use whites of eggs for top.

Pure, delicate, strong—Virot's Extracts.

SNOW PUDDING.

Mrs. W. B. Cushing.

Soak ½ package of gelatine ½ hour in 1 cup of cold water. Add 1½ cups of hot water and 1 cup of sugar. Beat whites of 3 eggs and beat into the gelatine, and keep cool. Flavor with lemon.

SAUCE.

Beat yolks of 3 eggs wtth ½ cup sugar and 1 teaspoonful of cornstarch. Scald 1 pint of milk; add to it the eggs till it thickens. Add salt and Virot's Vanilla, and let cool.

SPONGE PUDDING.

Mrs. H. D. Jarvis.

5 eggs, beaten separately.
1 pint of sweet milk.
½ cup of sugar.
¼ cup of butter.
½ cup of flour. Salt.

Scald milk; then stir in sugar and flour until it thickens. Add butter. When cool, add the yolks, then the whites of eggs. Bake ½ hour. Serve immediately with Hard sauce, filled with chopped nuts.

LEMON PUDDING.

Miss Prescott.

Mix 3 heaping tablespoonfuls of cornstarch into cold water until very thin. Pour on 3 coffeecups of boiling water. Boil till it thickens, stirring all the time. Then add 2 cups of sugar; grated rind and juice of 2 large lemons; 2 eggs, well beaten; salt to taste.

Butter a pudding dish and pour in. Bake 20 minutes. Serve cold with sugar and cream.

Equaled by none—Virot's Extracts.

ORANGE PUDDING.

Mrs. Franklin Burritt.

Take ⅓ box of gelatine and dissolve in ⅓ cup of cold water; then add ⅔ cup of boiling water, 1 cup of sugar and juice of 1 lemon. 1 cup of juice and pulp of orange, and the grated peel of 1 orange. Put this all together; put in cold place or on ice. When this begins to set, stir in the beaten whites of 3 eggs.

Custard to be served with the above : Take the yolks of 3 eggs; beat up with 3 tablespoonfuls of sugar, and stir into 1 pint of boiling milk. Cook over boiling water until it thickens. Whipped cream is preferred by many.

PRUNE PUDDING.

Miss Augusta G. Jones.

1 pound of prunes.
Whites of 4 eggs.

Soak the prunes over night. In the morning stone and stew them until tender, and sweeten to taste; then chop and add the beaten whites of eggs. Beat thoroughly and bake in well greased dish, 15 or 20 minutes in a moderate oven.

Serve with whipped cream.

PRUNE PUDDING.

Mrs. C. M. Rathbun.

1 pound of prunes.
1 cup of sugar.
Whites of 3 eggs.
¼ box of gelatine.

Soak prunes over night. In the morning remove stones; put the prunes in a porcelain lined kettle, with sufficient water to prevent burning, and cook until perfectly tender. Then add sugar, and let cool. When cold, press through a colander. Beat the whites to a stiff froth. Have the gelatine soaked in ½ cup of cold water for ½ hour; stand

For fastidious tastes—Virot's Extracts.

this over the fire until dissolved. Stir into prunes and whites of eggs; turn into mould and stand away to harden.

When ready to serve, pour around it a custard made from 1 pint of milk, yolks of 3 eggs, and 2 tablespoonfuls of sugar. Beat the eggs and sugar together until light; add to boiling milk, and cook until eggs begin to thicken—about 2 minutes, no longer, or sauce will curdle. Flavor very delicately with Virot's Almond.

TAPIOCA PUDDING.
Mrs. M. T. Dana.

4 tablespoonfuls of tapioca, soaked over night in 1 cup of water. Take the yolks of 4 eggs, beaten with 1 cup of sugar, and stir into 1 quart of boiling milk, which also contains the tapioca. Beat the whites of the eggs to a stiff froth. Put in a dish a small piece of butter and the whites of the eggs, pouring over it the cooked custard, which has been flavored to taste with Virot's Extract.

CHARLOTTE-RUSSE.
Mrs. A. R. Moore.

10 eggs.
1 cupful of sugar.
4 tablespoonfuls of wine.
1 tablespoonful of Virot's Vanilla Extract.
A little less than a package of gelatine.
1½ cupfuls of milk.
1 pint of cream.

Soak the gelatine in ½ cup of milk. Beat the yolks of eggs and sugar together, and put in a double boiler with the remaining milk. Stir until the mixture begins to thicken, then add the gelatine, and strain in a large tin basin. Place this in a pan of ice-water and when it begins to cool, add the whites of the eggs, well beaten, the wine, the flavoring and the whipped cream. Mix thoroughly, and pour into moulds that have been lined with sponge cake.

For dainty toilets—Virot's Perfumes, Toilet Waters, Sachets.

Set away to harden, and then cover with a thick covering of whipped cream. With the quantities given, 2 quart moulds may be filled. The lining may be one piece of sponge cake or strips of it, or lady fingers. The wine may be omitted.

The secret of the success of this rule is to have the cooked mixture *just* luke-warm, when the whites of eggs and the whipped cream are added. If it is too warm, it falls; if too cold, it lumps.

PINEAPPLE BAVARIAN CREAM.
Mrs. Joseph Brown.

1 can of pineapple, *not* grated.
½ box of Cooper's gelatine.
1 cup of sugar.
1 pint of cream.

Soak the gelatine in 1 cup of water. When dissolved, strain the juice from the pineapple; chop the pineapple fine. Put the gelatine, juice and pineapple together and scald. Set away to cool. When cool, whip the cream stiff; stir in mixture, and put into moulds. Serve with fruit juice sauce, or not.

PINEAPPLE SHORT-CAKE.
Mrs. P. H. Stevens.

1 cup of sugar.
1 cup of flour.
4 eggs.
3 tablespoonfuls of cold water.
Juice and grated rind of ½ lemon.
2 teaspoonfuls of baking powder.

This is baked in two layers, and grated pineapple, mixed with sugar, put between them. The top is covered with whipped cream.

Demand and Get—Virot's Perfumes and Extracts.

Ices.

BISCUIT GLACE.
Mrs. Ward Barnum.

Whip 1 quart of cream. Add to this yolks of 5 eggs and 1 cup of pulverized sugar, beaten together. Any flavoring may be used.

Maccaroons, dried, rolled and moistened with sherry, make it very nice. After stirring ingredients together, pour into a mould and pack in ice and salt, not stirring, but left to freeze slowly.

LEMON SHERBET.
Mrs. Lambert.

The rind of 2 lemons, scalded in 2 quarts of milk; the juice of 10 lemons, and 2 pounds of sugar. Let stand until sugar is dissolved. When milk is *thoroughly* cold, add the sugar and lemon juice. Strain before putting into freezer, so as to get out all the lemon rind. Then add the beaten whites of 4 eggs and 1 cup of powdered sugar, and freeze.

ORANGE SHERBET.
Mrs. A. S. Fox.

Juice of 10 oranges.
Juice of 6 lemons.
Grated rind of 2 oranges.
4 cups of sugar.
1 quart of water.

Cover the sugar with water; add the grated rind and boil for 5 minutes. Strain, and stand aside to cool. When cold add the orange and lemon juice and water. Freeze in a gallon freezer.

Price to suit all—Virot's Products.

CAFE PARFAIT.
Mrs. Palmer.

1 pint of cream.
1 cup of sugar.
1 spoonful of strong coffee.

Whip all together till thick. Put into a mould and pack in ice and salt, and let stand without stirring till frozen.

RASPBERRY ICE.
Miss Frisbee.

5 lemons; 2 cups of sugar; 1 quart of water; juice of 1 pint of raspberries.

Boil the sugar and water together, and when cold add the juice of the lemons and raspberries. Just before freezing, add the white of 1 egg, well beaten.

FROZEN PUDDING.
Mrs. A. R. Moore.

1 generous pint of milk.
2 cupfuls of granulated sugar.
A scant ½ cupful of flour.
2 eggs.
2 tablespoonfuls of gelatine.
1 quart of cream.
1 pound of French candied fruits (½ pound will do).
4 tablespoonfuls of wine.

Let the milk come to a boil. Beat the flour, 1 cup of sugar and the eggs together, and stir into the boiling milk. Cook 20 minutes; add the gelatine, which has been soaking 1 or 2 hours in water—enough to cover it. Strain and set away to cool. When cold, add the rest of the sugar and the cream, whipped until stiff. Have the fruit chopped fine, and soaked in the wine. Freeze the cream 10 minutes, then add the wine and fruit and finish freezing. Remove the beater, pack smoothly, and set away for several hours. When ready to serve, dip the tin into warm water, turn out the cream, and serve with whipped cream heaped around.

Something modern—Virot's Extracts.

Cakes and Cookies.

DOUGHNUTS.
Mrs. George E. Tiffany.

8 tablespoonfuls of sugar.
2 eggs, well beaten.
3 large tablespoonfuls of sour cream.
10 large tablespoonfuls of sour milk.
1 teaspoonful of soda.
Flour enough to make a soft dough. Flavor with Virot's Extract of Cinnamon or Nutmeg.

FRIED CAKES.
Mrs. R. H. Barnum.

2 eggs, beaten thoroughly; add 1 scant cup of sugar, and beat again. 6 tablespoonfuls melted butter, and beat again. 4 teaspoonfuls of baking powder sifted into the flour. Add 2 teacups sweet milk and a little salt. Mix very soft. Flavor with Virot's Extract of Nutmeg.

LAZY DOUGHNUTS.
Mrs. Owens.

½ cup of sugar; 2 eggs; 1 cup of sour milk; 6 level teaspoonfuls melted COTTOLENE; ½ teaspoonful soda.

Stir as stiff as possible with flour. Drop from a teaspoon into hot COTTOLENE, and fry brown. Dip spoon in the COTTOLENE each time, and they will not stick to the spoon.

Better than the Best—Virot's Extracts.

OLD-FASHIONED CRULLERS.
Mrs. R. E. Forbes.

3 eggs.
3 spoonfuls sugar.
1 spoonful of lard.
1 teaspoonful of baking powder.
A little salt.
Flour to make stiff enough to roll.

Roll ¼ of an inch thick. Cut in squares. Cut each square into strips from bottom to near top edge, representing five fingers. Slightly twist each strip, and bring all together at the end. This has a pretty effect after frying.

CRULLERS.
Mrs. Parker.

3 cups sugar; 6 eggs; 2 tablespoonfuls COTTOLENE; 3 teaspoonfuls of baking powder; 6 cups of flour.

Mix; cut ½ inch thick and drop into hot COTTOLENE. When brown sprinkle with sugar.

SPANISH BUN.
Mrs. Wm. H. Morgan.

1 egg, and the yolks of 3 eggs; ½ cup butter; 2 cups of coffee sugar; 2 cups of flour; 1 cup of milk; 3 teaspoonfuls of baking powder; 1 dessert-spoonful ground mixed spices.

Bake in a broad, shallow tin, in a moderate oven for 20 to 30 minutes.

Icing: To the well beaten whites of 3 eggs, add 1 cup of coffee sugar. Spread on the cake while it is warm. Then set in oven to brown nicely. Leave in pan until cold.

TIP-TOP CAKE.
Miss Katharine Cushing.

1½ cups of sugar; 1 cup of sweet milk; 1 egg; 2½ cups of flour; 1 tablespoonful of butter; 3 teaspoonfuls of baking powder. Flavor with Virot's Extract.

Pure, delicate, strong—Virot's Extracts.

SCOTCH SHORT-CAKE.
Miss Mary G. Bristol.

1 pound of flour; ½ pound butter; ¼ pound of sugar; pinch of salt.

Better to mix without water. Bake in a round cake ½ inch thick, pricked with fork and fluted edges. Break in pieces, and serve at 5 o'clock tea.

MRS. COMMONS' SPICE CAKE.

3 eggs; 1 cup of sugar; ½ cup of butter; ½ cup of sweet milk; ½ cup of molasses, into which put soda size of a bean; 2 cups of flour; 1 teaspoonful of baking powder; 1 coffeecup of raisins; 1 teacup of currants; 1½ teaspoonfuls of cloves; 2 teaspoonfuls of cinnamon.

Stir the butter and sugar together. Add the molasses and soda and spices, then the eggs, well beaten; then the milk; the flour, in which the baking powder has been sifted, and lastly the fruit dredged with flour.

SPONGE CAKE.
Mrs. C. M. Rathbun.

3 eggs; 1 large cup of sugar; 1 large cup of pastry flour; 1 teaspoonful baking powder; ⅓ cup of hot water; ⅓ lemon (juice and rind).

Beat eggs *very* light. Add gradually the sifted sugar; then the water and lemon, and lastly, the flour and baking powder. Bake in gem pans, or as a loaf.

SPONGE CAKE.
Mrs. L. N. Murray.

5 eggs; juice of 1 lemon; 1 small cup granulated sugar; 1 small cup of flour; pinch of baking powder.

Beat yolks and sugar to a cream. Add lemon juice; add the stiffly beaten whites of eggs, and put in flour and baking powder. Grease tins, and bake in a hot oven.

Equaled by none—Virot's Extracts.

WARM GINGER BREAD.

Miss Jean Rathbun.

1 egg, beaten lightly; ½ cup of molasses; 1 teaspoonful of soda; butter size of an egg, put into ½ cup of boiling water; 1 good cup of flour.

Mix thoroughly, and bake in a quick oven. Spice, if you wish.

NICE WARM TEA CAKES.

Mrs. George Barker.

1 cup of sugar; 2 cups of flour; 5 tablespoonfuls milk or water; 2 eggs; butter the size of an egg; 1 teaspoonful of baking powder.

Flavor with Virot's Vanilla. Drop from spoon on buttered tins.

LAYER CAKE.

Mrs. A. H. Marsh.

1 egg; ⅔ cup sugar; 4 tablespoonfuls cold butter, beaten to a cream. Add 1 cup sweet milk; 2 teaspoonfuls baking powder in 2 cups of flour.

Use cocoanut or English walnuts with the frosting.

GOLD CAKE.

Mrs. S. B. Durlin.

Yolks of 8 eggs.
1 scant cup of sugar.
½ cup of butter.
1⅔ cups of flour.
2 teaspoonfuls of baking powder.
Flavor with Virot's Extract.

Cream butter and sugar until very light. Beat yolks until very stiff, and stir through the butter and sugar. Put in milk, then flour, and stir hard. Oven moderate.

For fastidious tastes—Virot's Extracts.

SUNSHINE CAKE.
Mrs. S. B. Durlin.

Whites of 7 eggs.
Yolks of 5 eggs.
1 cup of granulated sugar.
1 cup of flour.
½ teaspoonful of cream of tartar.

Add a pinch of salt to the whites before beating. Sift, measure and set aside flour and sugar. Separate the eggs, putting whites in a mixing bowl, and the yolks in a small bowl, and beat until *very* stiff. Whip the whites about half; add cream of tartar and whip until *very* stiff. Add Virot's flavoring; add sugar to the whites, beat in; then add yolks; then the flour, which must be *folded* in very lightly. Bake in moderate oven 30 to 40 minutes.

WHITE CAKE.
Mrs. George Wiley.

½ cup of butter; 1 cup of sugar; ½ cup of cold water; 1⅔ cups of pastry flour; whites of 3 eggs; 2 teaspoonfuls of baking powder.

Flavor with Virot's Extract.

CHOCOLATE CAKE.
Mrs. W. W. Sloan.

1½ cups of granulated sugar; ½ cup of butter, rubbed to a cream; ½ cup of sweet milk; 2 cups of flour and 2 teaspoonfuls of baking powder, sifted together; 3 eggs, well beaten. Stir together thoroughly.

¼ pound Baker's Chocolate, scraped fine; add 5 tablespoonfuls of sugar and 3 tablespoonfuls of boiling water, stirring over the fire until smooth, then add to the mixture. Bake 20 minutes in a moderate oven.

WHITE FROSTING.

Whites of 2 eggs, beaten to a stiff froth. Boil 2 small cups of sugar till it hairs; beat into the whites until cold, and spread over the cake.

For dainty toilets—Virot's Perfumes, Toilet Waters, Sachets.

Then make a dark frosting the same way, only put in ¾ cup of grated chocolate. Stir until smooth, then spread over the white frosting.

CHOCOLATE LOAF CAKE.
Mrs. J. D. Maynard.

¼ cake of Baker's Chocolate; ¼ cup of milk; yolk of 1 egg. Boil these together until soft and smooth. Then add ¼ cup of butter; ¾ cup of sugar; ¼ cup of milk; 1 egg; 1 cup of flour; 1 small teaspoonful of soda, dissolved in a little hot water.

BLACK CHOCOLATE CAKE.
Mae Hayward.

1½ cups of granulated sugar; ½ cup of butter; 3 eggs; ¼ cup of sweet milk; 1 teaspoonful of soda; 1½ cups of flour; Virot's Vanilla.

½ cup of grated chocolate, cooked in ½ cup of milk, and when thoroughly *cold*, add to the cake mixture.

MRS. COMMONS' MAPLE SUGAR CAKES.

3 cups of maple sugar, grated; 1 small cup of butter; 1 cup of sour milk; 3 eggs; 1 teaspoonful of soda. Flour to make stiff enough batter for drop cakes.

QUEEN'S CAKE.
Mrs. A. S. Couch.

1 pound of dried flour; 1 pound of sugar; ¾ pounds of butter; 5 eggs; 1 nutmeg; 1 small wine-glass of wine; 1 small wine-glass of brandy; a gill of thin cream; 1 pound of raisins.

STRIPED CAKE.
Mrs. P. H. Stevens.

⅔ small cup of butter; 2 cups of sugar; whites of 5 eggs; 2½ cups of flour; 3 teaspoonfuls of baking powder; 1 cup of sweet milk. Bake in 2 square sheets.

Demand and Get—Virot's Perfumes and Extracts.

Take 3 tablespoonfuls of this batter. Add to it ½ cup of molasses; yolks of 2 eggs; 1 cup of raisins, seeded and chopped; ½ teaspoonful of cloves; 1 teaspoonful cinnamon; ½ cup of flour. Bake this in 1 layer.

Put 3 layers together with frosting, having dark one in the center.

FEDERAL CAKE.
Mrs. Geo. P. Isham.

1 pound of butter; 1 pound of sugar; 1 pound of flour; ½ pint of sour cream; 1 teaspoonful of saleratus; 4 eggs; 1 glass brandy; 1 pound of raisins; 1 nutmeg; ½ teaspoonful cloves.

ANGEL'S FOOD.
Mrs. Sophia White.

Whites of 11 eggs.
1½ tumblers of granulated sugar.
1 tumbler of flour.
1 teaspoonful of Virot's Vanilla.
1 teaspoonful of cream of tartar.

Sift the flour 4 times, then add the cream of tartar, and sift again, but have the right measure before putting in the cream of tartar. Sift the sugar and measure. Beat the eggs to a stiff froth on a large platter; on the same dish add the sugar lightly, then the flour *very gently*, and then the vanilla. Do not stop beating until it is in the pan to bake. Bake 40 minutes in a very moderate oven. Try with a straw. Do not open the oven until the cake has been in 15 minutes. Turn the pan upside down to cool, and when cold take out by loosening around the sides with a knife. Cut with a sharp knife. Use a pan that has never been greased, and have on the edges 3 or 4 projections about 2 inches deep, so that when turned upside down there will be a space between the pan and the table.

The tumbler for measuring must hold 2¼ gills.

Price to suit all—Virot's Products.

WEDDING FRUIT CAKE.

Mrs. M. S. Moore.

1 pound of butter; 1 pound of sugar; 1 pound of flour; 1 cup of molasses; 8 eggs, beaten separately; 4 wine-glasses of brandy; 6 pounds raisins; 3 pounds of French currants; 2 pounds of citron; 5 nutmegs; 2 tablespoonfuls of ground cloves; 2 tablespoonfuls of ground cinnamon.

Mix currants, raisins and citron with sifted flour. Stir butter and sugar to a cream; beat eggs very light; stir them alternately with the flour into the butter and sugar, stirring very hard. Add gradually the spices and liquor; stir the raisins and fruit into the mixture. Stir hard 10 minutes. Bake from 4 to 5 hours in a moderate oven. Ice the next day.

RAISIN CAKE.

Mrs. Wm. Risley.

1 cup of butter; 1 cup of sour milk; 3 eggs; 2 cups of sugar; 1 teaspoonful of soda; 2 teaspoonfuls baking powder; 3½ cups flour; 1 cup of stoned raisins. Flavor with Virot's Rose-water.

DRIED APPLE CAKE.

Mrs. W. B. Cushing.

2 cups of dried apples; 2 cups of molasses; 1 cup of butter; 1 cup of sour milk; 1 cup of brown sugar; 2 eggs; 1½ teaspoonfuls soda; 2 teaspoonfuls cinnamon; 2 teaspoonfuls of cloves; 1 nutmeg; 3 cups of flour.

Soak the apples over night, then chop and stew in molasses 1 hour. When cool, add the other ingredients.

JAM CAKE.

Miss Lizzie Lester.

1 cup of sugar; ½ cup butter (scant); yolks of 3 eggs; whites of 2 eggs; 1 teaspoonful of cinnamon; 1 teaspoonful

Something modern—Virot's Extracts.

of soda, dissolved; ½ cup of milk; 1½ cups of flour; 1 heaping teaspoonful of baking powder.

Beat thoroughly; then add 1 scant cup of jam, and beat well, Bake in layers or loaf.

MRS. DANIEL'S BUTTERNUT CAKES.

1 cup of butter; 2 cups of sugar; 3 cups of flour; 4 eggs; 1 cup of sweet milk; 3 teaspoonfuls of baking powder.

Add Virot's flavoring; and the last thing, add 1 coffeecup of butternuts, and bake in little tins. This will make 32 small cakes.

ENGLISH WALNUT CAKE.

Mrs. A. S. Fox.

1 cup of sugar; ½ cup of butter; ½ cup of milk; 2 eggs; 2 cups of flour; 1 heaping teaspoonful of baking powder; 1 cup of stoned raisins; 1 cup chopped walnuts.

Flour nuts and raisins before putting them in the cake.

HICKORY NUT CAKE.

Mrs. S. B. Durlin.

1 cup sugar; ½ cup butter; 2 cups flour; 2 teaspoonfuls baking powder; 2 eggs; ½ cup of sweet milk; 1 cup of chopped nuts.

HICKORY NUT MACAROONS.

Miss Ama L. Lester.

1 cup of brown sugar; 2 eggs, beaten together; 3 scant tablespoonfuls of flour; a pinch of salt; 1 cup of chopped nut meats.

To the eggs add sugar, then flour, then salt; then add the nuts. *Beat well.* Drop from a small spoon into well greased pan. Bake in a hot oven.

Better than the Best—Virot's Extracts.

KISSES.

Mrs. S. B. Durlin.

Whites of 4 eggs and ½ pound of pulverized sugar. Beat whites until *very, very* stiff (here lies the secret of success). Add 1 teaspoonful Virot's Vanilla, and then add the sugar. Drop on a *board* which has been thoroughly wet and covered with a paper which has also been wet; then bake in a cool oven ½ hour, or until they are well dried. Slip them off the board with a knife and put 2 together, the lower sides together. A couple of tablespoonfuls of chopped nuts—English walnuts, almonds or hickory nuts—the last thing before baking, is a great improvement. Make them of an oblong shape, which can easily be done.

SUGAR COOKIES.

Mrs. Franklin Burritt.

1 cup sugar; ½ cup butter; 1 egg; ½ cup of milk; 1 teaspoonful of baking powder; flour enough to make a stiff dough.

Roll as thin as possible. These are fine with or without caraway seed. (Seeds should be rolled).

SOUR CREAM COOKIES.

Mrs. H. D. Kirkover.

1 cup of butter; 1 cup of sugar; 3 eggs; 1 cup of sour cream; 1½ teaspoonfuls soda; flour enough to make a dough as soft as it can be rolled.

Sprinkle each cooky with a little granulated sugar before putting into the oven.

MOLASSES COOKIES.

Mrs. S. B. Durlin.

1 cup of molasses; 1 cup of brown sugar; 1 cup of lard and butter; 3 eggs; 1 teaspoonful each of cinnamon, ginger and soda.

Pure, delicate, strong—Virot's Extracts.

GINGER SNAPS.
Mrs. Wm. Parks.

1 cup of molasses; ⅔ cup of sugar; 1 scant cup of lard and butter; 1 egg; 1 teaspoonful of soda, dissolved in 1 tablespoonful of hot water; flour enough to mix stiff.

Boil molasses and sugar together for 5 minutes; then add the shortening and soda, and let cool a little before adding the flour. Ginger and spices to taste. Roll thin, cut and bake in a moderately hot oven.

SAND TARTS.
Miss Katherine Clark.

1 cup butter; 1½ cups sugar; 3 eggs, beaten separately; 1 tablespoonful water; 1 teaspoonful of baking powder.

Mix in sufficient flour to roll out thin, cut in squares. Brush the tops with white of egg, sprinkle sugar, cinnamon and chopped almonds on top, and bake.

MAPLE SUGAR COOKIES.
Mrs. D. R. Manley.

2 cups of *dark* maple sugar; ⅔ cup of butter; 1 egg; 1 cup of sour cream; ½ teaspoonful of soda.

Beat sugar, butter and egg together until light. Dissolve soda in cream, and add with sufficient flour to make a soft dough. Roll out and cut with round cutter. The more lumpy the sugar, the better the cookies.

FRUIT COOKIES.
Mrs. C. A. Clute.

2 eggs; 2 cups of brown sugar; 1 cup of butter; 1 cup of raisins; ½ cup of currants; ¼ pound of citron; ½ cup of sour milk, or ½ cup of cold coffee; 1 teaspoonful of soda; 3 teaspoonfuls of cinnamon; 1 teaspoonful of cloves. Flour enough to roll out as soft as possible.

Equaled by none—Virot's Extracts.

WALNUT WAFERS.

Miss Augusta W. Jones.

½ pint of brown sugar; ½ pint of walnut meats; 3 even tablespoonfuls of flour; ⅓ teaspoonful of salt; 2 eggs.

Beat the eggs, add the sugar, salt and flour, then the walnuts, chopped fine. Spread in buttered pans as thin as possible, and at equal distances put half walnuts. Bake in moderate oven. Divide into squares after cake has cooled a little.

ORANGE WAFERS.

Mrs. Jennie G. Cushing.

½ pound of sugar; ¼ pound of flour; 4 eggs, separate the whites and yolks, and beat very light; 1 lemon (use ½ the rind and all the juice); 2 teaspoonfuls of baking powder.

Drop from a spoon on buttered paper and bake in a quick oven. Spread the under side with orange marmalade, and place two together.

For fastidious tastes—Virot's Extracts.

Icings and Fillings.

PLAIN ICING.

Boil 1 cup of granulated sugar with 4 tablespoonfuls of water until it drops from the spoon in threads. Have ready the beaten white of 1 egg, and pour the syrup slowly into it, beating all the time. Use Virot's Favoring. Spread on cake while warm.

FROSTING WITHOUT EGGS.

1 cup of granulated sugar.
5 tablespoonfuls of water.
Boil for 5 minutes. Stir until it begins to boil. When done, set dish in cold water; add Virot's Flavoring. While cooling, stir or beat it continually. Frost cake while still warm.

CHOCOLATE FILLING.

Mrs. E. H. Potter.

1 cup of sugar; 5 tablespoonfuls of sweet milk; 2 tablespoonfuls shaved chocolate; butter size of a chestnut.

Boil about 3 minutes, and stir until cold. Put on the cake when both cake and filling are cold. If boiled a little too long, add a few drops of milk while stirring.

CHOCOLATE FILLING.

Miss Nellie C. Lake.

1 pint of sugar, with just enough water to wet it. Add whites of 3 eggs, beaten a very little; ½ cake of sweet chocolate, grated.

For dainty toilets—Virot's Perfumes, Toilet Waters, Sachets.

Set the pan into hot water, and cook 10 or 15 minutes. Take from fire, and when partly cold add as much grated cocoanut as you desire. Flavor with Virot's Vanilla. Spread between layers of cake, and sprinkle top and sides with cocoanut.

MAPLE SUGAR FILLING.

Mrs. Joseph Brown.

1 cup of granulated sugar; 2 cups of maple syrup; whites of 3 eggs.

Boil the sugar as for ordinary frosting. Put in maple syrup. Boil until it nearly hairs. Pour slowly on the beaten whites, and beat until very thick or nearly cold.

CARAMEL FILLING.

Mrs. F. B. Palmer.

1 cup of brown sugar; 1 cup of maple syrup; butter the size of an egg.

Boil until a soft candy. Add 2 tablespoonfuls of cream and stir until nearly cold. Then use.

MARSHMALLOW FILLING.

Mrs. Joseph Brown.

Frost both sides of layers with ordinary white frosting. Have fresh, soft marshmallows, pull them out flat and fit them on the frosting. Flavor with fresh lemon or Virot's Extract.

CREAM FILLING.

½ cup of flour; 2 eggs; 1 cup of sugar; ½ pint of milk.

Beat flour, eggs and sugar together, and stir into the boiling milk. Cook until it thickens, then stir until cool. Use Virot's Flavoring.

Demand and Get—Virot's Perfumes and Extracts.

FIG FILLING.

Mrs. S. B. Durlin.

¾ pounds of figs; 1 cup of raisins, chopped fine; make custard with 2 eggs; 2 tablespoonfuls of sugar; 2 tablespoonfuls of water.

Cook in double boiler; and when moderately cool, stir in the fruit and a generous tablespoonful of brandy.

APPLE FILLING.

Mrs. Jennie G. Cushing.

1 cup granulated sugar; 1 egg, beaten up light; 1 lemon, grate the rind and use all the juice; 2 large sour apples, grated.

Beat all together, and put on stove and boil a minute. Spread between layers of cake. Have the cake cold and the filling hot.

Price to suit all—Virot's Products.

Candies.

FRENCH CREAM.

To the white of 1 egg, beaten to a stiff froth, add 1 tablespoonful of cold water or sweet cream. Sift carefully XXX confectioner's sugar; stir into mixture gradually, keeping the mixture smooth, until you can mould with the fingers. Do not make it too stiff. This is the basis of the following recipes:

FRUIT CREAM.

Cut into small pieces dates, figs and citron. Add just enough of French Cream to hold the fruit together. Flavor with Virot's Violet Vanilla, stirring as little as possible to keep the fruit in shape. Make this into a flat cake about 1 inch thick and cut in cubes.

ORANGE FRUIT CREAMED.

Peel sweet oranges and separate into the smallest sections, care being taken not to pierce the fruit. Carefully remove the white skin. Around each section fold a layer of French Cream flavored with Virot's Orange.

ALMOND CREAMS.

Flavor a small quantity of French Cream with Virot's Bitter Almond. Roll into balls, and into top of each press a blanched almond.

ENGLISH WALNUT CREAMS.

Flavor French Cream mixture with Virot's Pistachio. Roll into balls, and place on top of each half an English walnut.

Something modern—Virot's Extracts.

CONFECTIONER'S CREAM CANDY.
Mrs. F. E. Cooke.

1 cup of cream, with Virot's flavoring. Roll and sift confectioner's sugar several times. Stir into cream all the sugar it will hold. Knead like bread, the longer, the better. Mould into any shape desired, and fill with nuts, or use for stuffing dates.

CONFECTIONER'S CREAM CANDY.
Mrs. F. E. Cooke.

Weigh 1 pound of confectioner's sugar. Break the white of 1 egg in a glass. In another glass put any kind of Virot's flavoring you desire, and combine with water to make the same proportion you have of egg. Now add water and flavoring to egg. Pour all into the sugar. Mix as for bread. Roll on smooth board; cut into squares, or work into any shape. By adding the yolk of egg, with a little sugar and Virot's Lemon flavoring, lemon cream is made. Any kind of fruit or nuts may be added.

A few drops of cochineal makes a pink candy.

CHOCOLATE CREAMS.
Mrs. F. E. Cooke.

Use either of the above confectioner's candy; let it stand several hours to harden. Then melt 1 cake of sweetened chocolate, by setting the dish into hot water. Take out one cream at a time on a fork and drop into melted chocolate; roll it until well covered, then slip from the fork upon waxed paper, and set aside to harden.

MOLASSES CANDY.
Miss Katharine A. Cushing.

2½ cups of molasses; 1 cup of sugar; 1 tablespoonful of vinegar; butter size of English walnut.

Boil 20 minutes, stirring cool on buttered pans, and pull until white.

Better than the Best—Virot's Extracts.

PEANUT CANDY.
Miss Mary J. Rathbun.

Shell, peel and chop 1 pound of peanuts. Put 2 teacups of granulated sugar into a hot sauce-pan over a slow fire, and stir constantly until dissolved. As the last specks of sugar are disappearing, stir in the peanuts quickly, and spread on buttered tins. While cooling, cut into squares.

WINTERGREEN TAFFY.
Mrs. Wm. Parks.

2 cups of coffee A sugar; ½ tablespoonful of vinegar; 2 tablespoonfuls of glucose.

Boil until it snaps when dropped into water. When partly cool add 10 drops of oil of wintergreen, and pull over a large nail. Pull into long strips and cut.

CONFECTIONER'S TAFFY.
Mrs. E. H. Potter.

2 pounds of sugar; ½ pound of glucose; 1½ cups Porto Rico molasses; 1 cup of butter.

Boil sugar and glucose together first; then add molasses. Boil until it will harden in water. Pour into buttered pans; when cool pull over hook until white. Add Virot's Vanilla while pulling. Cut in pieces and wrap in buttered paper. This will make 3 pounds of taffy. 3 dozen sheets of paper are required to wrap it.

CHOCOLATE CARAMELS.
Miss Ama Lester.

1 cup of sweet milk; 2 cups of molasses; 1 cup of sugar; butter size of an egg; ½ cake of Baker's chocolate.

Grate chocolate, and stir into the milk when boiling. Then add the other ingredients slowly. When it becomes brittle by dropping into cold water, pour into flat tins to cool.

Pure, delicate, strong—Virot's Extracts.

CREAM CANDY.
Mrs. R. B. Day.

2 cups of coffee C sugar, or 1 pound of maple sugar; 1 cup of thin cream.

Boil slowly 25 minutes, and pour over nuts. Do not stir after it begins to boil.

HONEY TAFFY.
Miss Marie L. Cushing.

4 cups of brown sugar; 1 cup of cream; 2 spoonfuls of vinegar; 1 spoonful of butter.

Boil until it hardens in water. Do not stir. Pull until of a very light color.

MAPLE BUTTER SCOTCH.
Miss Nicklis.

1 cup of maple syrup; 1 cup of granulated sugar; ½ cup of butter.

Boil until it snaps in water, then add 1 cup of hickory nuts. Pour into buttered tins and set away to cool.

FUDGES.
Miss Belle L. Tiffany.

2 cups sugar; 1 cup milk; ½ cake of Baker's chocolate.

Boil together until it will form a soft ball in water. Then add a tablespoonful of butter, and cook a short time. Take from the stove and stir until nearly hard. If nuts or cocoanut are to be added, they should be stirred in before pouring into pans to cool. If cream is used instead of milk, they will ramain soft for several days.

COCOANUT DROPS.
Mrs. Seldon E. Stone.

To 1 grated cocoanut, add ½ the weight of white sugar and the white of 1 egg. Rub to a stiff froth, mix well and drop on buttered white paper. Bake 15 minutes.

Equaled by none—Virot's Extracts.

PEPPERMINT CANDY.

Mrs. M. M. Fenner.

1 cup of granulated sugar; ¼ cup of water.

Put on stove and let it boil 1 or 2 minutes after it begins bubbling all over. It will string when right. Do not stir while boiling. When boiled, add 3 drops of peppermint oil and beat until it begins to turn slightly white, when drop quickly on marble or buttered paper.

PRALINES.

Mrs. A. R. Moore.

2 cups of sugar; ½ cup cream; 1½ cups of nuts (pecans preferred).

Boil sugar and cream until it will stay in the shape of a ball. Take off the stove and beat thoroughly, and when it begins to grain or sugar add nuts.

PANOCHA.

Mrs. P. R. Bradley.

4 cups of brown sugar; 1 tablespoonful of butter; 1 cup of milk; 1 teaspoonful of salt; 2 tablespoonfuls of Virot's Vanilla; 2 cups of chopped walnuts.

Boil the sugar, butter and milk until it drops hard in cold water. When done, pour in the vanilla and walnuts, and stir constantly until well mixed. Pour on a buttered platter and cut into squares.

For fastidious tastes—Virot's Extracts.

Jellies and Canning.

JELLIES.

All fruit jellies are made so much alike, that a few general directions are sufficient. For berries, currants, or grapes, heat the fruit, strain it and add 1 pound of sugar to each pint of juice. Crab-apple, quinces or apples must be stewed before straining; and to apple jelly may be added the juice of 4 lemons to 6 pints of apple juice. Crab-apple is improved by ⅓ pie-plant. For any jelly, boil the juice about 20 minutes. Add the sugar, and let it boil 2 or 3 minutes more. Always have the sugar hot when you put it in.

CRANBERRY JELLY.
Miss Augusta Jones.

1 quart of cranberries; 1 pound of sugar; ½ pint of water.

Wash the cranberries and put them on with the water to boil for 10 minutes, then mash and squeeze through a flannel bag. Return the juice to the kettle, add the sugar, boil rapidly, and continuously for about 10 or 15 minutes, or until it jellies, and turn out to cool.

ORANGE CONSERVE.
Mrs. Wm. H. Morgan.

5 pints of currant juice; 1½ dozen oranges; 9 pounds of sugar; 2 pounds of choice raisins, seeded.

For dainty toilets—Virot's Perfumes, Toilet Waters, Sachets.

Discard the ends of the oranges and the seeds, then cut into small pieces. Put the currant juice, raisins and oranges all together and boil 1 hour, then add the sugar and cook slowly ½ hour.

ORANGE MARMALADE.
Miss Mary G. Bristol.

12 sweet oranges (Valencia); 6 bitter oranges (Seville); 4 lemons; 8 pounds of sugar; 4 quarts of water.

After cutting the oranges and lemons in very thin slices, cover them with the water and let the whole stand 36 hours. Then boil 3 hours; add sugar, and boil 2 hours more. Just before taking off the fire add 1 wine-glass of whiskey to clear. So much depends on the size and sweetness of the oranges, that one must judge of the amount of sugar. Also, too much boiling makes the marmalade dark.

GINGER PEARS.
Mrs. Walter Finkel.

8 pounds of fruit; 4 pounds of sugar; ¼ pound of ginger root (green); juice of 4 lemons; 1 tumbler of water.

Rind of lemons to be cut thin and long. Peal and cut pears into thin slices (cannot be too thin). Boil ¾ of an hour. Use hard, green pears.

PRESERVED STRAWBERRIES.
Miss Augusta W. Jones.

1 quart of fruit; 1 quart of sugar.

Put into a kettle together on back of stove, and let them remain there until the sugar dissolves slowly. Then move to the front of stove and cook 10 minutes. Set kettle away in a cold place for the fruit to absorb and the juice thicken; then can. Do not cook more than 3 quarts at a time. Do not stir, but press down with spoon.

Demand and Get—Virot's Perfumes and Extracts.

BRANDY PEACHES.

Mrs. Lamira J. White.

18 pounds of loaf sugar to 20 pounds of whole peaches. Boil the peaches slowly till they become transparent; take them out and spread on dishes to cool. Boil the juice to a thick syrup; add 1 pint of brandy to 1 quart of syrup. Pour syrup over peaches hot.

UNFERMENTED GRAPE JUICE.

Miss Marie Cushing.

May be made for about 3 or 4 cents a quart bottle. Pick over the grapes, and almost cover with cold water in a porcelain-lined kettle. Heat slowly (mashing), and cook until all the juice is freed. Drain in jelly-bag. Measure the juice, and add ⅓ granulated sugar for each quart. Boil for 4 minutes and seal.

PINEAPPLE.

Miss Augusta W. Jones.

To can pineapple in its own juice without cooking: Cut up the fruit in dice or shred it. To 1 pound of fruit, 1 pound of sugar. Place in layers in a crock; leave over night. Put in glass cans, and fill to top; seal air-tight. Place in a dark place. Dip rubbers and covers in warm water. For a delicious flavor, add 1 dessert-spoonful of brandy to each quart jar.

TO CAN PIE-PLANT COLD.

Mrs. Robert Jones.

Wash stalks and cut into inch pieces. Fill cans lightly, and then fill up with cold water. Put on rubbers and tops *all* under water, to exclude air. Screw tops very tight.

Gooseberries and cranberries may be canned in the same way.

Price to suit all—Virot's Products.

PEACHES.

Pare and throw them into cold water. When you have enough to fill one or two jars, take them from the water, put them into a porcelain-lined kettle, cover them with boiling water, and stand on the back part of the fire where they will scarcely simmer, until tender. While they are cooking, make a syrup from 1 pound of sugar and 1 quart of water; stir over the fire until the sugar is dissolved, and then boil for 3 minutes. Lift the peaches carefully from the water, put them in the syrup, bring to a boiling point, and can as directed.

Can pears in exactly the same way.

CHERRIES.

Stone cherries; and if sour, allow ½ pound of sugar to every pound of cherries. If sweet, ¼ pound will be quite sufficient. Put into a porcelain-lined kettle, sufficient cherries to fill 2 jars, cover them with the sugar and stand aside for 2 hours, then bring to a boiling point, and can directly.

CURRANTS AND RASPBERRIES.

To each quart of large red raspberries, allow ½ pint of currant juice and ½ pound of sugar. Put the berries in a porcelain-lined kettle, add the juice and sugar, bring to boiling point and can.

Something modern—Virot's Extracts.

Pickles.

CANNED CUCUMBERS.
Mrs. Robert Jones.

Peel and slice thin medium sized cucumbers, sprinkle with salt and a little alum and let stand 2 hours. Drain, and put in jars, adding vinegar, pepper and a few whole mustard seeds (onions if desired). On top of the jar, when ready for sealing, add a dessert-spoonful of olive oil.

Good to serve with meat, fish or as a salad, and they will keep until June.

FLINT PICKLES.
Mrs. W. B. Green.

100 small cucumbers. 1 teacup of salt to a gallon of water, heated boiling hot. Pour over the cucumbers, let stand 24 hours. Repeat this twice. Then rinse them with cold water and wipe them dry. Line bottom of stone jar with grape leaves, pack cucumbers in layers with a few whole cloves and cinnamon sticks between. Cover with grape leaves, and fill the jar with vinegar.

PICKLES.
Mrs. F. B. Palmer.

1½ gallons of vinegar; 1 ounce of cloves; 2 ounces white mustard seed; 2 ounces of allspice; 2 ounces of alum; 8 ounces salt; several pieces of horseradish; 5 tablespoonfuls celery seed; 4 red peppers; 400 cucumbers put into a jar.

Better than the Best—Virot's Extracts.

Let the mixture come to a boil, pour over the cucumbers. Fill the jar with cold vinegar. Cover with grape leaves and tie paper tightly over. Ready for use in 3 weeks.

PICKLED CUCUMBERS.
Mrs. Franklin Burritt.

Take 300 small cucumbers; 1 pint of salt. Pour boiling water over them to cover. Repeat 3 mornings, then wash thoroughly in cold water and drain; put in jars. Take vinegar enough to cover pickles. Put in 1 ounce of alum, ½ ounce saltpetre and 1 coffeecup of sugar; boil together and pour over boiling hot. Some add 3 peppers, 3 onions and a few cloves.

GREEN TOMATO PICKLE.
Mrs. Kingsland.

2 gallons tomatoes, green and sliced; 12 good sized onions, sliced; 2 quarts of vinegar; 1 quart of sugar; 2 tablespoonfuls of salt; 2 tablespoonfuls ground mustard; 2 tablespoonfuls of black pepper, ground; 1 tablespoonful of allspice; 1 tablespoonful of cloves.

Mix all together and stew until tender, stirring often. Put up in glass jars.

CUCUMBER OIL PICKLES.
Mrs. C. D. Armstrong.

12 cucumbers; 3 onions; ½ cup of salt.

Slice cucumbers and onions thin, put in dish in layers with salt sprinkled over them. Let stand 2 hours. Rinse them off with cold water and place in cans, with the following poured over them : 1 pint of sharp, cold vinegar; tablespoonful or more, or even ½ cup olive oil (according to taste for oil); ½ cup of white mustard seed; ½ tablespoonful of celery seed.

These will be ready to serve in 3 hours.

Pure, delicate, strong—Virot's Extracts.

SWEET PICKLES.

Mrs. Franklin Burritt.

Take large ripe cucumbers (*thick-meated*); peel and cut in squares, soak in weak salt and water over night. Take out and drain. Then take ½ vinegar and ½ water, and boil until tender; remove and drain. Have ready a syrup, made of 4 quarts of cider vinegar and 4 quarts of granulated sugar; let them cook a short time, just enough for the syrup to penetrate.

PICALILLI.

Mrs. Lambert.

1 peck of green tomatoes, chop fine and drain; add 12 peppers and 4 onions, chopped; 2 quarts of vinegar; 1 cup white mustard seed; 2 cups brown sugar; 2 tablespoonfuls of cinnamon; 1 tablespoonful of cloves; 1 tablespoonful of allspice; 3 tablespoonfuls of salt.

Dissolve sugar and spices in vinegar. Mix thoroughly with the tomato; put up in glass jars cold.

CHOW-CHOW, OR ENGLISH PICKLE.

Mrs. S. G. Skinner.

4 heads of cauliflower; 2 quarts of small onions; 4 quarts of small cucumbers; 2 quarts of small tomatoes; (12 green peppers—which are cut in small pieces—if you like).

Salt the onions, cucumbers and tomatoes 24 hours. Divide the cauliflower, and salt separately, the same length of time. Drain thoroughly. Add the peppers, and put in a porcelain-lined kettle; cover with cold vinegar, not too strong, and boil 15 minutes. Drain and cool. Stir 1 cup of flour into some vinegar (about 1 quart) smoothly. Add ¾ pound of English mustard and boil, stirring *all the time*, to prevent burning. When cool, add 12 tablespoonfuls of

Equaled by none—Virot's Extracts.

olive oil, stirring constantly. Then add 1 ounce of turmeric, 1 pound of white mustard seed. Add enough good vinegar to cover. Mix thoroughly and bottle.

CHILI SAUCE.
Mrs. A. S. Couch.

30 large ripe tomatoes; 12 onions; 6 red peppers; 5 tablespoonfuls of salt; 20 tablespoonfuls of white sugar; 3 cups of vinegar.

Cook 2 hours. Do not skim.

CHILI SAUCE.
Mrs. W. B. Green.

24 large tomatoes; 6 large onions; 3 green peppers, all chopped fine. Add 8 teaspoonfuls sugar; 2 teaspoonfuls of salt; 2 cups of vinegar.

Cook slowly 3 or 4 hours.

SPICED CURRANTS.
Mrs. S. G. Skinner.

5 pounds of currants, stemmed and washed; 4 pounds of sugar; ½ pint vinegar; 2 tablespoonfuls each of cinnamon and cloves.

Put the vinegar and sugar in the kettle and heat. Add the currants and spices, and cook 1 hour, stirring to prevent burning. When done, rub through a wire sieve to take out the seeds.

GRAPE CATSUP.
Miss Marie L. Cushing.

Take 5 pounds of grapes, scald and strain. Add 2½ pounds of sugar; 1 pint of vinegar; 1 tablespoonful each of salt, pepper, cloves, cinnamon and allspice.

Boil till thick enough.

For fastidious tastes—Virot's Extracts.

MUSTARD PICKLE.

Miss Matilda Denton.

Take cauliflower, onions, cucumbers and string-beans. Put them in a brine for 3 days, changing brine each day. Take 1 gallon of vinegar, ½ pound of whole spices, and boil 20 minutes, Take 1 pound of mustard and ¼ pound of powdered turmeric bark; mix with cold vinegar, and put into the boiling vinegar. Allow all to boil 5 minutes, then pour over the pickle.

This will cover ½ bushel of pickle.

Household Hints.

For fruit stains, pour boiling water, hot soda water, or hot chloride water, through the spot.

Usually, an application of glycerine, mixed with yolk of egg, will cause tea stains to disappear. Or try dissolving ¼ pound each of chloride of lime and common soda in 3 quarts of boiling water. Dip the stains in this solution, and then wash in soft water.

Chocolate or cocoa stains must always be washed in cold water—never warm. Machine oil can be removed in the same way when fresh.

Grass stains can be removed by putting in alcohol or ammonia before the article is washed. Quickly put in warm suds, rub carefully with the hands till the spots disappear.

To keep the bright color of peas, beans or any green vegetable while cooking leave them uncovered. The above is also true of cranberries.

To remove tar, rub well with clean lard. Afterwards wash with soap and warm water.

Equal parts of ammonia and turpentine will take paint out of clothing. Saturate the spot as often as necessary, and wash in soap suds.

To make caramel: Put 1 cup of granulated sugar into an iron or granite sauce-pan, stir it over the fire till it melts and burns. As soon as it begins to smoke and boil add 1 cup of boiling water. Let it boil 1 minute, bottle and cork tightly. This is used for coloring soups, sauces and puddings.

Demand and Get—Virot's Perfumes and Extracts.

A piece of butter on a steel knife applied immediately after a bruise, will prevent a dark spot or lump.

Dry celery tops to use for soups.

When broiling steak, throw a little salt on the coals and the blaze from dripping fat will not annoy.

A piece of apple kept in the cake box will keep cake fresh and moist.

Brush a tough steak with plenty of olive oil and vinegar a few hours before cooking to make it tender.

Never mix salad with dressing until ready to use.

Lemon and salt will remove ink stains some times, and always remove iron rust. Put in the sun.

Brush white of egg over pastry to prevent custards soaking into crust.

Sugar for fried cakes should be dissolved in the milk to prevent them from absorbing lard.

To keep juice of fruit pies from running out while baking, put in small cornucopias of white stiff paper in openings in the upper crust.

Boil rice in a great deal of water; one gallon to a pound of rice is a good rule. After washing put it into boiling water which has been salted, and let it boil hard for twenty minutes, or less, if well cooked. Drain in a colander, put in oven five or ten minutes. Use the rice water for soup, adding ½ can of tomatoes, onion and parsley chopped fine. Pepper to taste.

Vegetables which grow above the ground may be cooked in salt water. Those under the ground in unsalted water.

To remove blood stains when it is impossible to use soap and cold water, make a thick paste of laundry starch and cold water. Plaster it over the stain and allow it to remain until perfectly dry. If one application does not answer, the second will be sure to remove it.

Price to suit all—Virot's Products.

Index.

	PAGE
Biscuit.	
Baking Powder,	45
Minute,	43
Butter Crackers,	44
Graham Wafers,	44
Breads.	
Brown,	52
Steamed,	53
Graham,	52
Indian Loaf,	52
Rye,	51
White,	50–51
Whole Wheat,	51
Cakes.	
Angel's Food,	80
Butternut,	82
Chocolate,	79
Black,	78–79
Dried Apple,	81
English Walnut,	82
Federal,	80
Fruit,	81
Ginger,	77
Gold,	77
Hickory Nut,	82
Jam,	81
Kisses,	83
Layer,	77
Macaroons,	82
Maple Sugar,	79
Queen's	79
Raisin,	81

Something modern—Virot's Extracts.

Scotch, - - - - - - 76
Spanish Bun, - - - - - 75
Spice, - - - - - - 76
Sponge, - - - - - - 76
Striped, - - - - - - 79
Sunshine, - - - - - - 68
Tea, - - - - - - 77

Candies.

Caramels, Chocolate, - - - - - 90
Cocoanut Drops, - - - - - 92
Cream Candy, - - - - - - 92
Creams, Almond, - - - - - 89
    Confectioner's, (2) - - - - 90
    Chocolate, - - - - - 90
    English Walnut, - - - - 89
    French, - - - - - 89
    Fruit, - - - - - 89
Fudges, - - - - - - 92
Maple Sugar Scotch, - - - - - 92
Molasses, - - - - - - 90
Orange Fruit, Creamed, - - - - 89
Panocha, - - - - - - 93
Peanut, - - - - - - 91
Peppermint, - - - - - 93
Pralines, - - - - - - 93
Taffy, Confectioner's, - - - - 91
    Honey, - - - - - 92
    Wintergreen, - - - - - 91

Canning.

Cherries, - - - - - - 97
Currants and Raspberries, - - - - 97
Grape Juice, - - - - - 96
Peaches, - - - - - - 97
Pears, - - - - - - 97
Pie-plant, - - - - - - 96
Pineapple, - - - - - 96

Cheese.

Cheese Croquettes, - - - - - 39
    Fondu, - - - - - 39
    Souffle, - - - - - 39
    Straws, - - - - - 39

Better than the Best—Virot's Extracts.

Cookies.

Fruit,	84
Ginger,	84
Maple Sugar,	84
Molasses,	83
Orange Wafers,	85
Sand Tarts,	84
Sour Cream,	83
Sugar,	83
Walnut Wafers,	85

Doughnuts.

Crullers,	75
Old Fashioned,	75
Doughnuts,	74
Lazy,	74
Fried Cakes,	74

Eggs.

Devilled,	38
Escalloped.	38
Omelet, French,	37
with Smoked Beef,	37
Scallop,	38
Scrambled Eggs,	37

Fish.

Baked,	16
Boiled,	16
Codfish Balls,	18
Cutlets,	16
Lobster Croquettes,	18
Minced Fish,	18
Salmon Loaf,	17
Southern Shrimp, etc.,	20
Turbot,	17

Gems, etc.

Corn Pone,	50
Gems, Graham,	47
Indian Meal,	48
Johnny Cake,	50
Muffins,	46
Corn,	47
Potato,	47

Pure, delicate, strong—Virot's Extracts.

Pop-overs,	43–46
Rye Puffs,	46
Sally Lunn,	43

Griddle Cakes.

Buckwheat,	49
Flannel,	49
Indian Meal,	49
Rice,	49
Wheat,	48
Waffles,	48

Household Hints.

Household Hints,	103–104

Ices.

Biscuit Glace,	72
Cafe Parfait,	73
Frozen Pudding,	73
Raspberry,	73
Sherbet, Lemon,	72
Orange,	72

Icings and Fillings.

Apple,	88
Caramel,	87
Chocolate,	87–88
Cream,	87
Fig,	88
Frosting without Egg,	86
Maple Sugar,	87
Marshmallow,	87
Plain,	86

Jellies.

Aspic,	40
Cranberry,	94
General Directions,	94

Meats.

Baked Hamburg Steak,	23
Beef Omelet,	22
Brick of Beef,	22
Boudins,	23

Equaled by none—Virot's Extracts.

Chicken, Creamed,	26
Croquettes,	27
Dressing for,	25
Pillau,	26
Roast,	24
Liver, Stewed,	24
Royal Scallop,	25
Sweetbreads, Fried,	24
Turkey, Dressing for	25
Roasted,	24
Tongue de Terrapin,	22
Veal Cutlets,	24
Loaf,	23

Oysters.

With Brown Sauce,	19
Cocktail,	21
Creamed,	21
Croquettes,	20
Escalloped,	21
Fried,	19
Gumbo,	20

Pickles.

Chilli Sauces,	101
Chow-Chow,	100
Cucumbers, Canned,	98
Pickled,	99
Oil,	99
Flint,	98
Grape Catsup,	101
Green Tomato,	99
Mustard,	102
Picalilli,	100
Pickles,	98
Sweet,	100
Spiced Currant,	101

Pies.

Apple,	61
Cream Pie-plant,	62
Currant,	60
Custard, Maple,	62
Pineapple,	61

For fastidious tastes—Virot's Extracts.

English Mince Meat, - - - - 63
Lemon, - - - - - - 60
Snow, - - - - - - 60

Preserves.
Brandy Peaches, - - - - - 96
Ginger Pears. - - - - - 95
Orange Conserve, - - - - - 94
    Marmalade, - - - - .. 95
Strawberries, - - - - - 95

Puddings.
Charlotte Russe, - - - - - 70
Chocolate, - - - - - - 66
    Steamed, - - - - - 66
Cup, Steamed, - - - - - 66
Custard, Cream, - - - - - 67
    French, - - - - - 67
Dumpling, Strawberry, - - - - - 65
Frozen, - - - - - - 73
Graham, - - - - - - 64
Healthful, - - - - - - 66
Lemon, - - - - - - 68
Mountain Dew, - - - - - 67
Orange, - - - - - - 69
Pineapple Bavarian Cream, - - - 71
    Short Cake, - - - - - 71
Plum, - - - - - - 64
Prune, - - - - - - 69
Snow, - - - - - - 68
Sponge, - - - - - - 68
Suet, - - - - - - 65
Tapioca, - - - - - - 70
Yorkshire, - - - - - 41

Rolls.
Rolls, - - - .. - - - 44
Parkerhouse, - - - - - - 44
Rusks, - - - - - - 43-45
Cinnamon Buns, - - - - - 46

Salad Dressing.
Cream, - - - - - - - 55
Dressing, - - - - - - 54-55
French, - - - - - - 55
Mayonnaise, - - - - - - 54

For dainty toilets—Virot's Perfumes, Toilet Waters, Sachets.

Salad.

Celery, - - - - - - -	56
Chicken, - - - - - -	57
Orange, - - - - - -	58
Peanut, - - - - - -	59
Potato, - - - - - -	55–56
Sweet Bread, - - - - -	57–58
Tomato, - - - - - -	57
Tongue, - - - - - -	58
Veal, - - - - - - -	56
Waldorf, - - - - - -	59

Sandwiches.

Celery, - - - - - -	40
Delicious, - - - - - -	40

Sauces.

Bearnaise, - - - - - -	29
Brown Sauce with Mushrooms, - - -	28
Cream Horseradish, - - - - -	29
Hollandaise, - - - - -	29
Mustard Dressing, - - - - -	30
Spanish Sauce, - - - - -	28
Tartare, - - - - - -	30
Tomato, - - - - - -	30

Soup.

Asparagus - - - - - -	10
Black Bean, - - - - -	10
Celery, - - - - - - -	11
Clam Chowder, (3) - - - -	11–12
Corn, - - - - - - -	12
Julienne, - - - - - -	12
Mullagatawny, - - - - -	13
Onion, - - - - - -	13
Oyster - - - - - -	13
Pea, (split) - - - - -	14
Potato, - - - - - -	15
Salsify, - - - - - -	13
Stock, - - - - - - -	9
White, - - - - -	9
Tomato, - - - - - -	15
Clear, - - - - -	15
Vegetable, - - - - - -	14

Demand and Get—Virot's Perfumes and Extracts.

Tarts.

Banberry, - - - - - - 61
Orange, - - - - - - 62

Vegetables.

Asparagus on Toast, - - - - - 31
Beans, Baked, - - - - - 36
    Sour, - - - - - - 32
Corn Fritters, - - - - - 32
    Oysters, - - - - - 31
Egg Plant, Fried, - - - - - 32
Kal Dolma, - - - - - 33
Mushrooms, Stewed, - - - - 33
Onions, Baked, - - - - - - 35
Oyster Plant Fritters, - - - - 34
Potato Croquettes, - - - - - 34
    Sweet, - - - - 34
Potatoes, Delmonico Hashed, - - - - 33
    Silverthorne, - - - - 34
Rice Cakes, - - - - - - 35
    Boiled, - - - - - - 104
    and Tomatoes, - - - - - 35
Tomatoes, Fried, - - - - - 36
    Scalloped, - - - - - 35
    Stuffed, - - - - - 36

Yeast.

Yeast, - - - - - - - 50

Price to suit all—Virot's Products.

www.ingramcontent.com/pod-product-compliance
Lightning Source LLC
Chambersburg PA
CBHW031406160426
43196CB00007B/923